The Complete Color Guide To Aurora H.O. Slot Cars

1st Edition

Compiled and Edited By
Bob Beers

Echo Point Books & Media, LLC
Brattleboro, Vermont

Published by Echo Point Books & Media
Brattleboro, Vermont
www.EchoPointBooks.com

All rights reserved.
Neither this work nor any portions thereof may be reproduced, stored in a
retrieval system, or transmitted in any capacity without written permission
from the publisher.

Copyright © 2000, 2024 by Bob Beers

All correspondence should be directed to:
   Bob Beers
   PO Box 255
   Monroe, CT 06468
   email: rbeers@snet.net
   or
   Robert Molta
   2201 Teall Ave,
   Syracuse, NY 13206
   email: bob@slotcarcentral.com

Special care was taken to ensure the accuracy of the
contents of this publication; however, the author can
assume no responsibility for the accuracy of its contents.

Model Motoring® is a registered trademark of Model Motoring, Inc.
AFX® is a registered trademark of Tomy Ind.
Aurora® is a registered trademark of Cinemodels, Inc.
All trademark names used herein are used for the purpose of
identification and the benefit of the trademark holder.
No infringement of trademarks is intended.

The Complete Color Guide to Aurora H.O. Slot Cars
ISBN: 978-1-64837-419-7 (paperback)

Photography, Design & Layout by Herb Clay
Graphics by Herb Clay and George Helf,
         Earth Spice Studio
         Stamford, CT
         ww.earthspicestudio.com

Cover design by Kaitlyn Whitaker

Dedication:

This book is dedicated to the memory of our son
Jason Loring Beers
and to my endearing wife Joni,
my daughter Alyssa, and my son Jeremy
In addition, a dedication goes out to all
the great friends I have met as a result
of Aurora H.O. slot car collecting.

Contributions:

There are many individuals whom I have met, that have helped me and taught me to appreciate the hobby. I would like to thank them all for their assistance through the years in making this compilation as complete as possible.

Dan Esposito (New York): Dan's perseverance helped to make me realize that this book had to be done. Dan also has made me a better person by helping me see that friendship, honesty, and fairness are more important than having another piece for the collection. Good cars at great prices can always be found. Good friends, with no strings attached can't. I know I found one in Dan.

Tom Stumpf (New York): The AFX Line is almost entirely from Tom's collection. Tom, a great friend, braved a snow and ice storm in February to be a part of this book. Several key pieces were loaned to me. I couldn't have done it as well without him.

Carl Mendez (New York): Carl sold Tom Stumpf his AFX collection so that Tom could lend it to me. Okay, that's not exactly how it happened. Carl's former cars are again, a big part of the book. Carl taught me to believe in AFX at a time when I was only interested in Tjets.

Dave Lockwood (Connecticut): Dave loaned his plastic kit collection and other key pieces for the photo shoots. He has also been a wealth of information to me throughout the years.

Mark Strickrodt (Connecticut): Mark took a dark and dingy basement and turned it into a showplace for me to proudly display my Aurora H.O. slot car collection. When it comes to pride in workmanship and true friendship, Mark is first rate.

Roy Manarin (Canada): Roy has been a friend from the first day we met. He realized my sincere love for the Aurora Plastics Company and its HO slot cars. I in return realized his great contribution to our hobby by unknowingly rescuing the last remnants of the legacy of Aurora. We all can thank him for the documentation and prototypes he has brought forward.

John Morstadt (New York): John loves accessories and his list helped me cross reference many part numbers in that section.

Ralph Phillips (Connecticut): Ralph is a large scale slot car collector and contributed 1/32 scale Aurora pieces to be included in this book.

Harrison Woodrow (Pennsylvania): Harry started Model Motoring, Inc. He has always been a friend and when he got started in the hobby, supported my HOCARS shows tremendously. Harry took a personal risk starting his company and it has paid off. His products and services to the hobby are second to none. He sponsors many HO racing events and has always been a generous contributor. Check his website, www.model-motoring.com and mail for a catalog of current offerings today. Send snail mail to: Model Motoring, Inc. 360 Constance Drive, Warminster PA 18974

Former Aurora Employees (Worldwide): There are many of whom I have spoken to or met in the past 13 years of collecting. I thank them for their generosity both towards my personal collection and the preservation of the legacy of Aurora. To a person, they all echo one comment and that is that there never was a greater company to work for than Aurora. My only regret in life is that I never had the foresight to apply for a job there as a young adult.

Table of Contents

Chapter	Title	Pages
Chapter 1	Introduction	5
Chapter 2	Playcraft Highways	6–9
Chapter 3	Vibrators	10–18
Chapter 4	Thunderjets	19–55
Chapter 5	Ford/Aurora Grand Nationals	56–64
Chapter 6	"O" Gauge	65–73
Chapter 7	Cigarbox	74–77
Chapter 8	Speedline/Speedsters	78–83
Chapter 9	Other Scales	84–90
Chapter 10	Xlerators	91–94
Chapter 11	AFX	95–136
Chapter 12	Prototypes and Promotional Items	137–143
Chapter 13	Track & Accessories	144–148
Chapter 14	Chassis	149–151
Chapter 15	Sets	152–156
Chapter 16	Catalogs and Paperwork	157–160

Chapter 1
Introduction

I, like most other baby boomers of the '60's, can remember the first time I was introduced to Aurora HO slot cars. I was 10 years old in 1961 and my first set was a Vibrator set. I played with it and it often interfered with the TV set, so I had to stop in the evenings. Heck, my set interfered with my neighbor's TV set and they called to complain more than once. The house I grew up in had radiant heat (in the floor) and it was quite comfortable on the floor racing slot cars for hour after hour. My friends and I added new cars, trucks, and accessories to our pit cases. We had a big track at a friend's house and I spent many days in his basement expanding the layout and adding HO trains to it. Mid-teens I discovered girls and the slot cars were history. After the usual life stuff, and a tragedy (my wife, Joni and I lost our son, Jason, tragically in 1989), I found myself looking for something to occupy my free time. Most hobbies help take your mind off life's issues and problems and put you in a place where there is nothing but bliss. This hobby has done just that for me. My family will tell you, I am consumed by it. I have asked my wife Joni, our 13 year old daughter Alyssa, and 8 year old son Jeremy to add their comments to my passion.

From my wife, Joni: My message is to all the Aurora widows. Be kind to your poor misguided overgrown boys. For some reason they derive great pleasure from these silly little cars. See how they smile when they pay unheard of sums for their rare gems? It makes them happy and isn't that what's really important?

From my daughter, Alyssa: Personally, I think that slot cars are a waste of time and rot your brain. I've been known to call my dad (and his friends) dorks or losers. Now that I think about it, as long as it keeps my dad happy (and occupied) then it's cool with me. Plus, if he's in a good mood, I'm more likely to get what I want. :)

From my son, Jeremy: I think my dad likes them because a lot of other people like them except me. He collects them and I think that is silly. I think it is smart to collect *Poke'mon* cards. I don't look forward to going on long van trips to HO slot car shows with my dad and his friends, Danny, Tom, and Carl. They always make me squeeze in a little spot and they pile slot cars on top of me. Carl keeps taking my blanket.

Knowledge of the history of the Aurora Plastics Company, it's employees, and it's products are my pride and my passion. This knowledge and the amazing wealth of slot car related things I have acquired over the years, have prompted me to compile this book. Like any other hobby, sharing it with others is the greatest joy. I hope you enjoy seeing it and learning about it as much as I have. Let Bob Beers and Slot Car Central be your guide!

Availability

Availability is the key to how common or rare a particular car or item is. I have chosen not to include prices as a value for items for a number of reasons. The price is very subjective. It can be based on geographical location of the sale, as well as the demand for the item. With the surge of the internet and on line auctions, collectibles have never been as readily available as they are now. Aurora H.O. slot cars are no exception. They are auctioned off daily and some can go for astronomical numbers. As the demand subsides the price drops dramatically. H.O. slot car shows are experiencing an upswing in popularity. The prices seem to be stable and the demand for rarer cars is rising. The range I show for the availability will cover an item from common to rare. If your item shows as a 1 or 2 in the rarity guide then it is very desirable and you should inquire to a seasoned collector as to the current market values. Look for these numbers next to the item to establish it's rarity.

Rarity index:

-5- very common
-4- common
-3- desirable
-2- very desirable
-1- rare
-0- very rare

Chapter 2
Playcraft Highways

If there is a "father" of the HO slot car, it has to be Englishman, Derek Brand. Not only did he invent the thunderjet, but also the original vibrator cars for Playcraft Toys Limited, in England back in the late 1950's. Derek invented the AC powered 'vibrator' motor while experimenting with a motor small enough to power a 'OO' gauge slotted powered car. In England 'OO' gauge is 1/76th scale, between true 1/87th (HO) scale and 1/48 (O scale). Today this seems sensible as Aurora took liberties with "true scale" throughout their production years. No company in the US could be found to satisfy requirements for a license to manufacture the Model Motoring system. Instead, the "HO" slot system license was fist sold to British Metoys, Playcraft division. Derek, in addition to developing the vibrator system, also had a hand in the Aurora AFX design and Tyco's 440 chassis design. Playcraft Highways was a short lived as a product over in England for a few reasons. In 1959, at a Hobby and Toy Expo in England, Aurora's executives, saw the product and immediately saw the future in it in the US market. Aurora bought the rights to the Model Motoring line, and kept the name, and in 1960, began to market sets in the US. Playcraft sold the Highways product in England. The country was dominated by 1/32nd scale slot cars and HO never took hold. After a few years, Playcraft stopped making sets, (they only marketed two), and Aurora opened a sales office in England. Playcraft's history into the development of the Aurora AC vibrator line is shown here with a list of their products and production dates.

3101 Jaguar XK140 open sports car 1959
(BODY/INTERIOR/BOOT)

☐ lemon/green/tan 3   ☐ white/green/tan 3   ☐ red/green/tan 3   ☐ blue/red/tan 3   **typical box**

The Jaguar is the predecessor to the Aurora vibrator #1541. This one has slightly different shades to the plastic, and there are thicker sections,

3102 Mercedes Benz open sports car 1959
(BODY/INTERIOR/TOP COVER)

☐ lemon/black/tan 3   ☐ white/red/tan 3   ☐ red/black/tan 3   ☐ blue/red/tan 3   **typical box**

The Mercedes is the second car Aurora chose to manufacture. The vibrator counterpart is #1542. This Playcraft version has different shades to the plastic and it is thicker upon visual inspection when the chassis is removed.

3103 Chevrolet Impala Sedan 1959
(BODY/TOP)

☐ lemon/white 1   ☐ white/red 1   ☐ blue/white 1   **typical box**
☐ white/lemon 1   ☐ red/white 1   ☐ white/blue 1   ☐ green/red 1   ☐ red/green 1

The Chevrolet Impala is a highly sought after car today. You would think, being an American car, Aurora would have manufactured it. I'm sure Derek Brand designed it into the slot car line in order to entice an American toy company into licencing it. The problem with the Chevy is that it is a manufacturing nightmare. There are (9) separate pieces all glued together to form the sides and top of the car. This gives a great two tone look to the car, but manufacturing was not as simple as the one piece molded bodies of the Jaguar and Mercedes. Consequently, the '58 Impala was short lived. Many examples today show a darker glue line around the fenders and other areas. This is common and should not detract from the car's desirability too much.

3201 Ford Lorry open stake truck 1959
(CAB/BED)

☐ *lemon/lemon 2* ☐ *red/red 2* ☐ *white/blue 2* ☐ *blue/blue 2*　　*typical box*
not shown: ☐ *lemon/white 2* ☐ *red/white 2* ☐ *white/yellow 2* ☐ *white/red 2* ☐ *blue/white 2*

The Lorry (English for truck) is another manufacturing problem. Too many pieces to fabricate. The design was an English Ford and Aurora chose to do their own line of trucks. The Lorry is (4) separate molded pieces glued together. There should be a spare tire under the back deck and a small round cardboard tube was packed with the truck to keep it from rattling around in the box. Often there is a stain near where the spare was located due to discoloring over the years. This should not be too much of a value deterrent due to the scarcity of the piece.

Playcraft Highways—Track & Accessories

☐ *3001*　*9" Curved Track*
☐ *3002*　*6" Curved Track*
☐ *3003*　*9" Straight Track*
☐ *3004*　*7" Straight Track*
☐ *3005*　*5" Straight Track*
☐ *3006*　*Junction Turnoff*
☐ *3007*　*9" Terminal Straight Track*
☐ *3701*　*Speed Control*
☐ *3501*　*Guard Rail*
☐ *3502*　*Bridge Supports*
☐ *3503*　*Sundries (Parts & Wires)*

#1 Set Oval Track

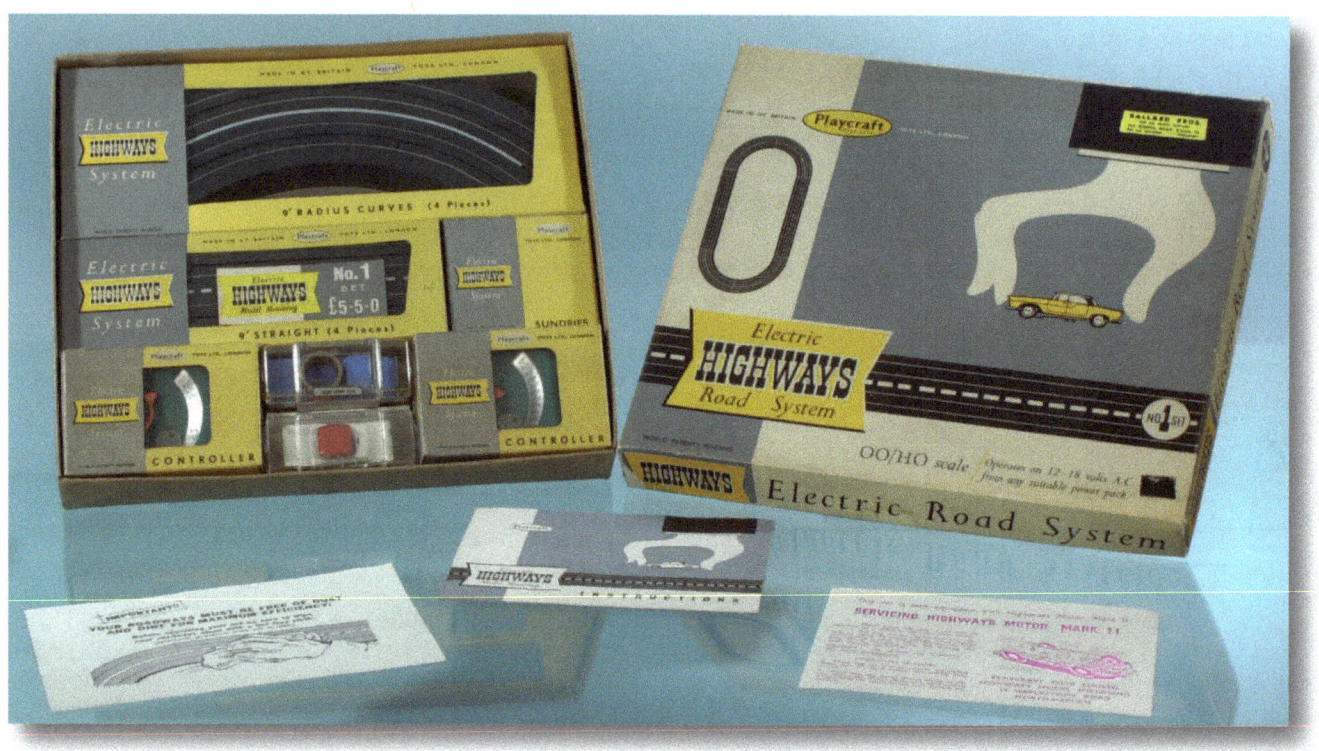

#2 Set Figure 8

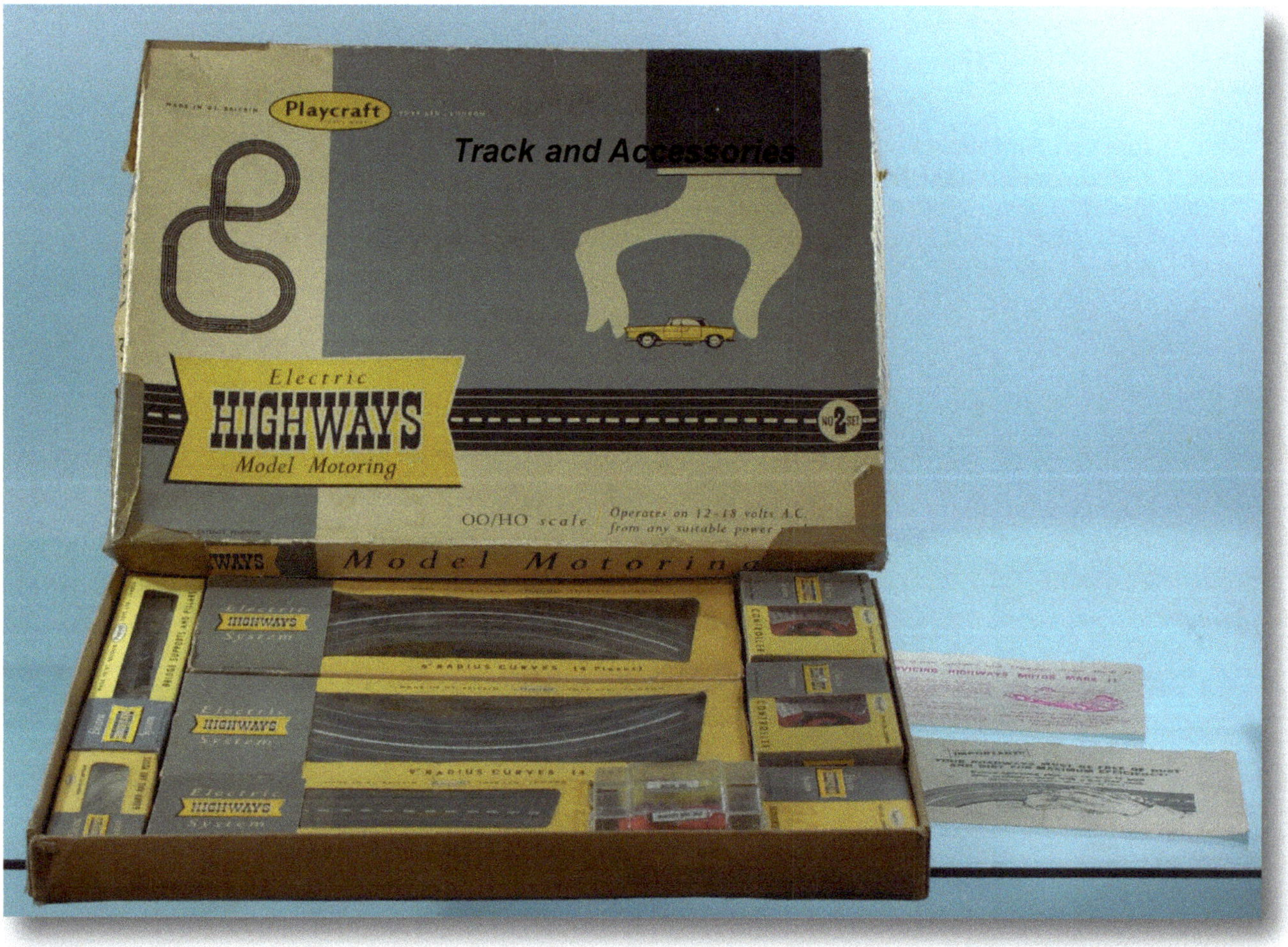

Track and Accessories

Assorted Track & Accessories Pieces

Assorted Track Pieces

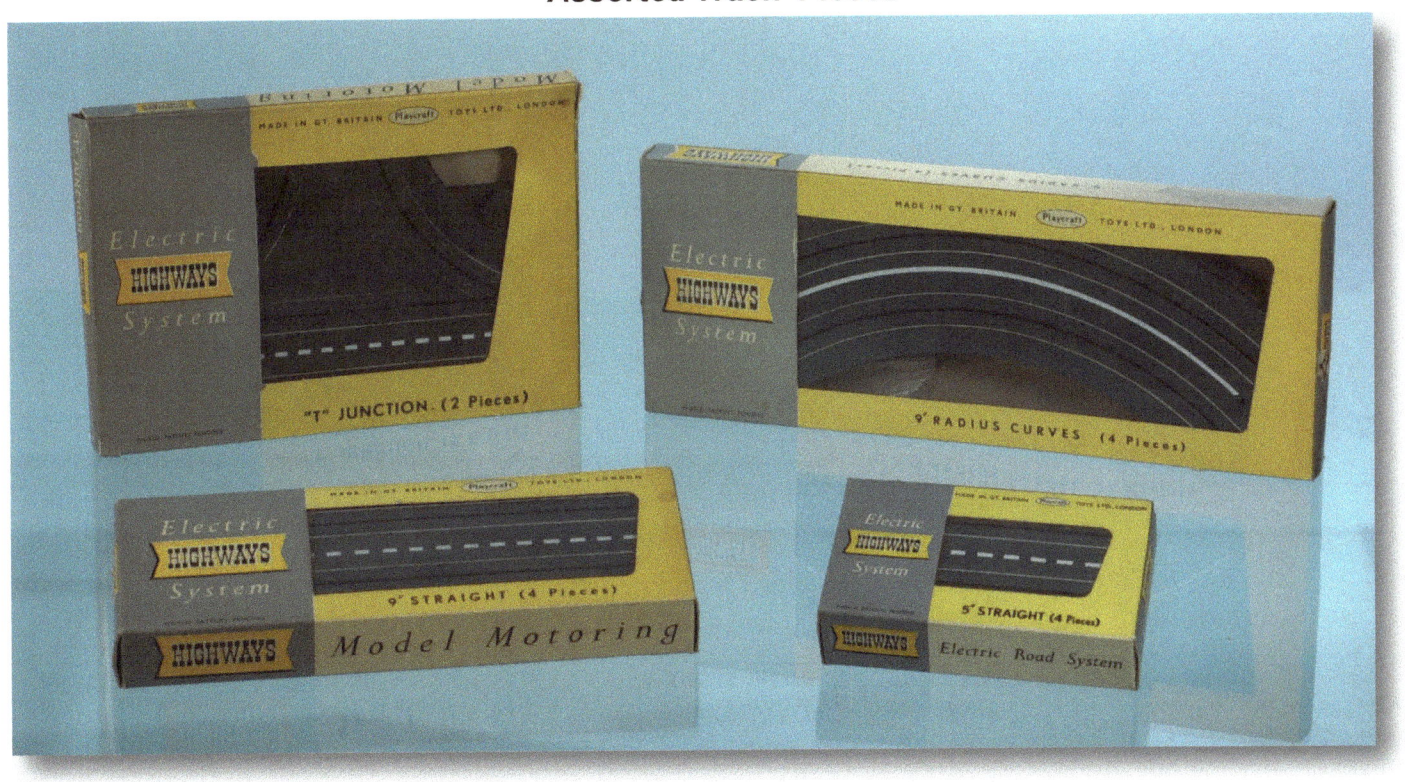

Chapter 3 Vibrators

The cars were packaged in a (2) car blue and yellow box or a (2) piece clamshell box. Early sets came in brown cardboard shipping cartons and the cars were packed in the blue and yellow boxes. The vibrator chassis is unique as it is a vibrating reed and electro magnet turning a drum between the rear wheels.

1541 Jaguar XK140 convertible 1960-62
(BODY/INTERIOR/BOOT)

☐ lemon/red/black 5   ☐ lemon/tan/black 5   ☐ red/tan/black 5   ☐ wine/black/tan 2   ☐ wine/tan/black 2
☐ white/black/tan 5   ☐ white/black/red 5   ☐ white/red/black 5   ☐ blue/tan/black 4   ☐ tan/red/black 4
☐ green/tan/black 4   ☐ green/black/tan 4   ☐ black/red/tan 3   ☐ dark gray/red/black 3   ☐ light gray/red/black 3

This is the first car that Aurora came out with under their own name. It is very similar to the Playcraft Highways Jaguar XK140 but this one used a different type of color in the plastic along with some differences in the mold. The body is a one piece mold with sprayed on silver bumpers. Often the windshield or the driver are missing from the car.

1542 Mercedes Benz 300SL convertible 1960-62
(BODY/INTERIOR/TOP COVER)

☐ lemon/red/black 5   ☐ lemon/tan/black 5   ☐ white/red/black 5   ☐ blue/black/tan 4   ☐ green/black/tan 4

Not Shown:
☐ lemon/lemon/black 5
☐ white/black/red 5
☐ light gray/tan/black 3
☐ black/brown/tan 3

☐ wine/black/tan 5   ☐ red/black/tan 5   ☐ red/tan/black 4   ☐ red/black/tan 2

☐ dark gray/red/black 3   ☐ light gray/red/black 3   ☐ tan/red/black 4   ☐ black/red/tan 3

This is the second car that Aurora came out with under their own name. It is very similar to the Playcraft Highways Mercedes but this one used a different type of color in the plastic along with some differences in the mold. The body is a one piece mold with a sprayed on rear silver bumper and a glued on front bumper. Often the windshield or the driver are missing from the car.

1543 Corvette convertible 1960-62
(BODY/COVE MOLDING/INTERIOR)

- lemon/black/red 2
- lemon/silver/red 3
- lemon/red/red 3
- wine/silver/red 2
- red/silver/tan 3
- white/silver/red 3
- white/black/black 3
- white/black/red 2
- blue/silver/black 2
- blue/silver/tan 2
- green/silver/tan 2
- tan/silver/red 3
- drk grey/silver/blk 2
- drk grey/silver/red 2
- metallic grey/silver/red 0

not shown:
- red/white/lemon 3
- green/lemon/tan 2
- light grey/silver/red 2
- black/silver/red 1

This is the first car that Aurora released that was designed for them. The Corvette convertible is a fairly nice scale replica of the real thing right down to the cove molding and the familiar Corvette checkered flag emblems. The body is a one piece mold with sprayed on silver bumpers. The windshield and driver are often missing from the car. The driver's head and upper body torso are smaller than those in any other Aurora car. A common problem with used versions of the Corvette is that the front bumper has been cut away to allow for clearance for the Thunderjet 500 chassis pickup shoes after the stock vibrator chassis has been discarded.

1544 Thunderbird 1960-62
(BODY/TOP (PO=PAINTED OUTSIDE))

- lemon/lemon 3
- lemon/black (PO) 5
- lemon/black 5
- wine/black/tan 2
- wine/tan/black 2
- red/red 3
- wine/black 3
- red/black 5
- wine/tan 3
- red/tan 4
- white/black 5
- bright white/black (PO) 4
- white/tan 4
- green/black 3
- green/tan 2
- blue/black 3
- blue/tan 3
- blue/tan (PO) 2
- black/tan 1
- black/tan (PO) 1

Continued on next page.

1544 Thunderbird 1960-62 (continued)
(BODY/TOP)

Not shown:
☐ metallic gray/black 0

☐ light grey black 3 ☐ dark grey/black 3 ☐ light grey/tan 2 ☐ dark grey/tan 2

The Thunderbird, which most replicates a 1958 model, is a popular body style. The body is a one piece mold with sprayed on silver bumpers. It came in several different body and top combinations, with the same color combo being the most desirable. The metallic gray is the toughest variation of this car. The interior is cut out of the car. The top can be found either painted outside or painted inside with the variation painted on the outside being the earlier one.

1545 Jaguar XK140 Hardtop 1961-62
(BODY/INTERIOR/TOP)

☐ lemon/red/black 4 ☐ lemon/red/lemon 3 ☐ red/tan/black 4 ☐ wine/tan/black 2 ☐ red/tan/red 3

☐ white/red/black 4 ☐ blue/tan/black 3 ☐ green/tan/black 3 ☐ tan/red/black 4 ☐ light grey red/black 3

☐ tan/red/tan 3

This body style is identical to #1541 with the exception that it has a one piece hardtop glued on it. The top is painted on the inside and there is no driver inside. Same color top and body combinations are the most desirable.

1546 Mercedes Hardtop 1961-62
(BODY/INTERIOR/TOP)

☐ lemon/red/lemon 3 ☐ lemon/red/black 4 ☐ red/tan/red 3 ☐ red/tan/black 4 ☐ tan/red/tan 3

☐ white/red/black 4 ☐ bright white/red/black 4 ☐ black/red/black 1 ☐ blue/tan/black 3 ☐ green/tan/black 3

not shown: ☐ red/black/black 4   ☐ white/red/tan 3   ☐ tan/red/black 4
          ☐ wine/tan/black 3   ☐ light gray/red/black 3   ☐ dark gray/red/black 3

This body style is the same as #1542 with the difference being a one piece hardtop. The top is painted from the inside. There is no driver inside. Same color top and body combinations are the most desirable.

1547 Corvette Hardtop 1961,62
(BODY/INTERIOR/TOP)

- ☐ lemon/red/lemon 2
- ☐ lemon/red/black 2
- ☐ red/tan/red 2
- ☐ red/tan/black 3
- ☐ white/red/black 3
- ☐ blue/tan/black 2
- ☐ green/tan/black 2
- ☐ tan/red/tan 2
- ☐ dark gray/red/black 2
- ☐ light gray/red/blk 2
- ☐ black/red/black 0

This body style is identical to #1543. There is a one piece hardtop painted on the inside. There is no driver in this car. Same body and top color combinations are very desirable. The cove color is always silver.

1548 '62 Ford Sunliner Convertible 1962
(BODY/INTERIOR/BOOT)

- ☐ lemon/red/black 4
- ☐ push chassis 4
- ☐ lemon/black/white 4
- ☐ red/tan/black 4
- ☐ white/red/black 4
- ☐ push chassis 4
- ☐ white/black/tan 4
- ☐ tan/black/white 4
- ☐ push chassis 4
- ☐ tan/red/black 4

(2) piece clamshell box

The Ford body style was used on four different vibrator cars so Aurora made a lot of use out of the molds. This car was sold as a low cost push car with a plastic chassis for use on train layouts. Several turned up in the early '90's on the west coast of the USA. The windshield and driver are commonly missing from this car in used condition. The front and rear bumpers are molded in the body and sprayed silver.

1549 '62 Ford Galaxie Hardtop 1962
(BODY/INTERIOR/TOP (PTL=PAINTED TAIL LIGHTS))

☐ lemon/red/lemon 3   ☐ lemon/black/lemon 3   ☐ red/tan/red 3   ☐ white/red/black 4   ☐ white/black/black 4

☐ tan/black/tan 3   ☐ tan/black/tan (PTL) 3   ☐ tan/black/black 4

This is a one piece body with the bumpers molded in and sprayed silver. The top is painted on the inside. The same body and top color combination is more desirable. Earlier versions of this car had the rear tail lights painted red. There is no driver in this car.

1550 '62 Ford Country Squire Station Wagon 1962
(BODY/INTERIOR/TOP (CC=CUSTOM CHROME, PO=PAINTED OUTSIDE))

☐ lemon/red/lemon (CC) 2   ☐ lemon/red/lemon 4   ☐ lemon/brown/lemon 3   ☐ lemon/red-lemon/lemon 4   ☐ lemon/red-lemon/lemon (PO) 3

☐ white/red-white/black 3   ☐ white/red-white/tan 3   ☐ tan/red-tan/tan (PO) 3   ☐ tan/red-tan/tan 4

☐ red/tan-red/red 3   ☐ red/tan/red 3

This is a one piece body with the bumpers molded in and sprayed silver. The top is painted on the inside on the later versions and painted on the outside on earlier versions. Earlier versions of this car had the rear tail lights painted red and the door handles detailed in chrome spray.

1551 '62 Ford Pick Up Truck 1962
(BODY/INTERIOR)

☐ lemon/red 3   ☐ red/tan 3   ☐ white/red 3   ☐ tan/red 3

This truck was a one piece molded body with a glued on rear section for the tail gate. The front grille was sprayed on silver paint. The top was one piece and painted on the inside. There is a simulated black tonneau cover over the bed, even though the catalog shows detail of tools in the bed.

1552 '62 Ford Police Car 1962
(BODY/INTERIOR/TOP)

☐ lemon/black/black 2   ☐ lemon/black/white 2   ☐ tan/black/black 2   ☐ tan/black/white 2

☐ red/black/black 2   ☐ red/black/white 2   ☐ white/black/black 2   ☐ white/black/white 2

This car uses the same one piece body as #1547. The top can be found painted on the outside on earlier versions and painted on the inside on later versions. The earlier ones had a inoperable light glued on the top while the later ones had a top with the light molded in. All police cars should have a silver star on each door and the words "POLICE" in black letters across the trunk. The stars are commonly worn off from handling.

1553 Hot Rod Roadster 1962
(BODY/INTERIOR)

☐ lemon/red 3   ☐ lemon/black 3   ☐ red/tan 3   ☐ white/red 3   ☐ blue/tan 2

☐ green/tan 2   ☐ tan/black 3   ☐ tan/red 3   ☐ black/red 1

The Hot Rod was a Vibrator car for only one year. This car had four chrome pipes on each side and the doors were smooth with NO protrusions. The roadster has a chrome windshield frame and chrome roll bar, along with a driver. The chassis has the more desirable (3) spinner knock off chrome hubs that were only supplied with this car and #1554. There was a decal sheet packed in the box.

1554 Hot Rod Coupe 1962
(BODY/INTERIOR)

☐ lemon/red 3   ☐ lemon/black 3   ☐ red/tan/ 3   ☐ white/red 3   ☐ white/black 3

☐ blue/tan 2   ☐ green/tan 2   ☐ tan/red 3   ☐ black/red 1

The Hot Rod was a Vibrator car for only one year. This car had four chrome pipes on each side and the doors were smooth with NO protrusions. The coupe has a chrome windshield frame and a top attached to it. The top is always the same color as the body. The chassis has the more desirable (3) spinner "knock off" chrome hubs that were only supplied with this car and #1553. There was a decal sheet packed in the box.

1580 International Truck Tractor 1961
(BODY/TOP)

☐ lemon/black 3   ☐ red/red 0   ☐ red/black 3   ☐ wine/black 1   ☐ white/black 3

☐ green/black 2   ☐ blue/black 2   ☐ light gray/black 2   ☐ dark gray/black 2

The International Truck Tractor has a sprayed on front grille and a top with a molded in horn. There is a square hole in the back to accept the square pin in the articulated trailers (#1585, #1586). The top is black on all of the Semi's that I have seen, with the exception of the red one. This was released with the same color top as the body probably towards the end of the Vibrator production run. (*See #1363 in the Aurora Thunderjet chapter.*)

1581 Mack (COE) Truck Tractor 1961

This truck was listed in the Aurora Model Motoring Order Sheet dated January 1, 1961. It was due to come out in April, but there have been no reported sales and none have been found to exist.

1582 Ford Dump Truck 1961
(CAB/BED)

- ☐ lemon/gray 3
- ☐ lemon/green 3
- ☐ red/gray 3
- ☐ white/green 3
- ☐ white/gray 3
- ☐ blue/gray 2
- ☐ green/gray 2
- ☐ tan/green 3
- ☐ light gray/green 2
- ☐ dark gray/green 2

not shown: ☐ red/green 3 ☐ blue/green 2 ☐ green/green 2 ☐ tan/gray 3 ☐ light gray/gray 2 ☐ dark gray/gray 2

The Dump Truck has dual yellow hubs in the back and single hubs in the front. The hubs contain lug nut detail and are preferred over the standard dimpled hubs on the Thunderjet trucks. The underside of the body contains a square cutout just forward of the rear post. This allows for clearance for the vibrating mechanism on the top of the chassis.

1583 Ford Stake Truck 1961
(CAB/BED/STAKES)

- ☐ lemon/gray/gray 3
- ☐ lemon green/gray 3
- ☐ lemon/green/green 3
- ☐ red/green/green 3
- ☐ red/gray/gray 3
- ☐ white/green/gray 3 
- ☐ tan/gray/gray 3
- ☐ tan/green/green 3
- ☐ tan/green/gray 3
- ☐ green/gray/gray 1
- ☐ blue/gray/gray 1
- ☐ dark/gray/gray/green 2
- ☐ light gray/green/green 2
- ☐ dark gray/green/green 2

note: All cab colors have (4) variations of different bed and stake combinations.

The Stake Truck has (2) sets of dual yellow hubs in the back and single hubs in the front. The hubs contain lug nut detail and are preferred over the standard dimpled hubs on the Thunderjet trucks. The underside of the body contains a square cutout just forward of the rear post. This allows for clearance for the vibrating mechanism on the top of the chassis.

1584 Stake Body Trailer 1961

This Stake Body Trailer was listed in the Aurora Model Motoring Order Sheet dated January 1st 1961. It was due to come out in June, but there have been no reported sales and none have been found to exist.

1585 Box Body Trailer 1961
(BODY/FRAME)

☐ gray/gray 5   ☐ green/green 5   ☐ gray/green 5

Not Shown:
☐ green/gray 5

The Box Body Trailer has a square pin in the front and it is articulated. When the pin is in the tractor bed the rear wheels of the trailer turn when the tractor turns. This is accomplished with a couple of thin rods located under the trailer bed. The trailer has the more desirable yellow dually hubs with the raised lug nuts.

1586 Van Body Trailer 1961
(BODY/FRAME)

☐ green/green (logo) 1   ☐ green/green 5   ☐ gray/gray 5   ☐ gray/green 5   ☐ gray/gray (logo) 1

not shown: ☐ green/gray 5

The Van Body Trailer has a square pin in the front and it is articulated. When the pin is in the tractor bed the rear wheels of the trailer turn when the tractor turns. This is accomplished with a couple of thin rods located under the trailer bed. The trailer has the more desirable yellow dually hubs with the raised lug nuts. The Aurora logo trailer has the words "Hobby Kits" around the logo. There are reports that there is one that says "Model Motoring" but I have not seen it.

Chapter 4
Thunderjets

In 1963, under a lot of pressure from customers that had a hard time tuning and controlling the finicky Vibrators, Aurora introduced the **Thunderjet series** of HO slot cars. These were far more superior to the Vibrators in many ways. They were DC powered and no longer were HO slot cars contributing to static on TV sets. You could run a vibrator on a tjet track but you would burn out a tjet running it on an AC current Vibrator power pack. The Tjets were easy to service. Simple gearing and replaceable parts made this car fun to drive. The Vibrator was a thing of the past, as the Tjets were widely accepted as the HO slot car standard of the industry. Millions were sold within a matter of a few years. By 1965 Aurora had sold over 25,000,000 HO slot cars. Aurora sponsored promotions where customers could trade in their older Vibrator cars for Tjets and some of the bodies were even interchangeable. In 1964 Aurora started to use bubble pack packaging on their cars and accessories. This helped the store owners keep down the pilfering and also displayed the items well. One drawback is that bubble packs take up a lot of valuable space to display. Aurora packaging is a key factor in the rarity of an item.

1351 (1251) '63 Ford Galaxie 500/XL Convertible 1963-69
(BODY/RUGS/SEATS/BOOT)

- lemon/red/black/black 1
- yellow/red/black/black 2
- turquoise/gray/black/black 2
- red/tan/black/tan 2
- red/tan/black/black 2
- white/red/black/black 2
- white/dark blue/lt blue/lt blue 1
- white/red/black/red 1
- tan/black/red/white 2
- tan/brown/tan/brown 2

Not Shown:
- yellow/brn/wht/blk 2
- red/black/tan/black 2
- wht/lt bl/dk bl/lt bl 1
- lmn/red/tan/red 1
- trq/blk/wht/wht 2
- tan/brn/tan/wht 2
- grn/blk/lt grn/blk 1

- olive/tan/black/tan 1
- olive/tan/black/black 1
- gray/black/red/black 2

The Galaxie convertible has a one piece molded body with a chrome front and rear bumper as separate pieces. The windshield, drivers head, and bumpers are commonly missing from a car found in used condition. That will substantially reduce the value. Cut rear wheel wells are a common problem also, due to the tightness of the rear tires to the inside of the body.

1352 (1252) '63 Ford Galaxie 500/XL Hardtop 1963-69
(BODY/RUGS/SEATS/TOP)

- lt yellow/brown/white/lt yellow 2
- yellow/brown/white/brown 1
- yellow/red/black/black 2
- red/black/tan/red 2
- red/black/tan/black 2
- white/dark blue/white/lt blue 1
- white/red/black/black 2
- olive/tan/black/black 1
- green/lt green/black/green 1
- green/lt green/black/black 1

Continued on next page.

1352 (1252) '63 Ford Galaxie 500/XL Hardtop 1963-69 (continued)
(BODY/RUGS/SEATS/TOP)

☐ turquoise/gray/black/black 2
☐ tan/black/tan/black 2
☐ tan/red/black/black 2
☐ gray/black/red/black 2

Not shown:
☐ lemon/red/tan/red 1
☐ white/lt blue/dk blue/lt blue 1
☐ tan/brown/tan/tan 2
☐ yellow/black/red/yellow 2
☐ white/black/red/red 2
☐ tan/black/red/tan 2
☐ turquoise/gray/black/turquoise 2
☐ white/lt blue/dark blue/white 1
☐ olive/tan/black/olive 1
☐ red/tan/black/black 2
☐ tan/brown/tan/brn 2
☐ gray/black/red/gray 2

The Galaxie Hardtop has a one piece molded body with a chrome front and rear bumper as separate pieces. It is identical to #1351. The top is commonly missing from a car found in used condition. That will substantially reduce the value. Cut rear wheel wells are a common problem also, due to the tightness of the rear tires to the inside of the body.

1353 (1253) '63 Ford Fairlane Hardtop 1963-69
(BODY/INTERIOR/TOP)

☐ lemon/red/black 1
☐ yellow/red/black 3
☐ pale yellow/red/black 2
☐ white/dk bl/lt bl 2
☐ white/red/black 3

☐ trq/black/white 2
☐ trq/grey/black 3
☐ red/tan/red 3
☐ red/black/red 3
☐ red/black/black 3

☐ olive/lt green/ blk 2
☐ green/lt green/black 2
☐ tan/brown/brown 2
☐ tan/red/tan 3
☐ tan/red/black 3

Not Shown:
☐ lemon/red/lemon 1
☐ yellow combinations 3
☐ turquoise combo's 3
☐ red combinations 3
☐ green combinations 2
☐ olive combintions 2

☐ pale ylw/brown/brown 2
☐ gray/red/black 2
☐ gray/black/gray 2
☐ gray/red/gray 2

The Fairlane Hardtop has a one piece molded body with a chrome front and rear bumper as separate pieces. The top is painted on the inside and is commonly missing from a car found in used condition. That will substantially reduce the value. Cut rear wheel wells are a common problem also, due to the tightness of the rear tires to the inside of the body.

1354 (1254) '63 Ford Falcon Sprint Hardtop   1963-69
(BODY/INTERIOR/TOP)

- ☐ lemon/red/black 1
- ☐ yellow/red/black 3
- ☐ pale ylw/brn/brn 2
- ☐ pale ylw/red/blk 2
- ☐ turquoise/gray/black 3
- ☐ red/black/black 3
- ☐ red/black/tan 3
- ☐ red/black/red 3
- ☐ red/tan/red 3
- ☐ olive/gray/black 2
- ☐ white/red/black 3
- ☐ white/dk blue/lt blue 1
- ☐ white/dk blue/dk blue 1
- ☐ white/red/red 1
- ☐ green/lt green/green 1
- ☐ tan/brown/brown 2
- ☐ tan/brown/black 3
- ☐ tan/black/tan 3
- ☐ gray/black/gray 2
- ☐ gray/red/gray 2

Not Shown: ☐ red/tan/black 3

The Falcon Hardtop has a one piece molded body with a chrome front and rear bumper as separate pieces. The top is painted on the inside and is commonly missing from a car found in used condition. That will substantially reduce the value. Cut rear wheel wells are a common problem also, due to the tightness of the rear tires to the inside of the body.

1355 (1255) '63 Thunderbird Sports Roadster   1963-69
(BODY/RUGS/SEATS)

- ☐ yellow/red/black 3
- ☐ turquoise/gray/black 3
- ☐ turquoise/red/black 3
- ☐ red/tan/black 3
- ☐ white/red/black 3
- ☐ white/dk blue/lt blue 1
- ☐ tan/brown/black 3
- ☐ slate/red/black 1
- ☐ olive/tan/black 2
- ☐ gray/red/black 0

Not Shown: ☐ tan/green/black 3   ☐ slate/black/gray 0

The Thunderbird Roadster is a one piece body with separate front and rear chrome bumpers. The windshield and drivers upper body are separate pieces and are often missing from a used car. A shortened front screw post is a sure way to tell if this car is an original Tjet or a Cigarbox car. The grey variation came both ways.

1356 (1256) '63 Corvette "Sting Ray"   1963-72
(BODY)

☐ yellow 3   ☐ turquoise 3   ☐ red 3   ☐ white 3   ☐ blue 2
☐ green 2   ☐ olive 2   ☐ tan 3   ☐ slate 1   ☐ gray 1

The Corvette Sting Ray is a one piece body with chrome front and rear bumpers as separate pieces. The glass is a separate piece also. This was one of the most popular Tjets of all time and was manufactured for many years.

1357 (1257) '63 Buick "Riviera"   1963-69
(BODY)

☐ yellow 3   ☐ turquoise 3   ☐ white 3   ☐ red 3   ☐ blue 2
☐ green 2   ☐ tan 3   ☐ green 2   ☐ slate 1   ☐ gray 1

The Riviera was the only Buick that Aurora manufactured. Not surprising for a company that had obvious favoritism toward Ford in it's product line. The Riviera is a one piece molded body with separate front and rear chrome bumpers. The glass is a separate piece also. The front screw post can be shorter in the Cigarbox versions that do not command as high a value as the tjets.

1358 (1258) XKE Jaguar   1963-70
(BODY)

☐ yellow 3   ☐ turquoise 3   ☐ red 3   ☐ white 3   ☐ blue 2
☐ green 2   ☐ olive 2   ☐ slate 1   ☐ tan 3   ☐ gray 1

Continued on next page.

1358 (1258) XKE Jaguar 1963-70 (continued)
(BODY)

Not shown:
☐ black (painted) 2

☐ black (molded) 2 ☐ black w/factory repair ticket 0 ☐ tan w/Holland box (note the text) 2

The Jaguar is a one piece molded body with separate chrome bumpers front and rear. The "glass" is a separate piece.

1359 (1259) Indianapolis Racer 1963-70
(BODY/NUMBER)

☐ lemon #2 2	☐ yellow #1 4	☐ yellow #2 4	☐ yellow #3 4	☐ tan #2 4
☐ turquoise #1 4	☐ turquoise #3 4	☐ turquoise #5 4	☐ turquoise #11 4	☐ white #1 4
☐ red #5 4	☐ red #7 4	☐ red #7 4	☐ red #11 4	☐ gray #3 1
☐ tan #2 4	☐ tan #3 4	☐ tan #3 4	☐ olive #3 1	☐ olive #5 1

Interestingly enough, the first pictures of this car that Aurora showed had the Vibrator knock off type Hot Rod hubs on the car. Early tjet versions of this car may have been supplied with those hubs. There are many different color combinations of the ball with the numbers and the drivers interior area. The body is one piece with a drivers head and a small windshield attached. The rarity on these cars is based more on the actual color than the ball color combinations. There have been reports of a blue Indy racer but I have never seen one documented. Different shades of white exist and have been called cream. They do not command a higher price than the white ones. There is a question often asked about why Aurora didn't use numbers like 4, 8, 9, 10 on their early cars. The answer is simply this. Any number that closes on itself such as 8, would require (2) masking processes to accomplish. From a manufacturing and production standpoint, Aurora chose to produce cars in the easiest numbers manufacturable (1, 2, 3, 5, 7, 11, 13).

1360 (1260) Indianapolis Racer (Plated)   1963-69
(BODY/NUMBER)

☐ silver #1 3   ☐ silver #2 3   ☐ silver #3 3   ☐ silver #5 3   ☐ silver #7 3

Not shown:
☐ gold #1 3
☐ gold #2 3
☐ gold #3 3
☐ gold #5 3

☐ silver #11 3   ☐ silver #13 3   ☐ gold #11 3   ☐ gold #13 3

This car is identical to #1359 except that it is the first car that Aurora used their new metallizing process on. They held up well through the years and the base color of the car varies.

1361 Gran Prix Racer   1965-70
(BODY/NUMBER)

☐ yellow #5 3   ☐ yellow #7 3   ☐ green #2 1   ☐ green #7 1   ☐ turquoise #3 3

☐ red #2 3   ☐ red #6 3   ☐ red #7 3   ☐ red #7 3   ☐ white #5 3

☐ tan #2 3

The Gran Prix Racer has a very fragile chrome roll bar, motor, and pipes piece that mounts behind the driver. This piece is almost always missing or broken. Many combinations of color and number were made. They never had a ball around the number as is shown in the 1965 Color Catalog. The tires are treaded truck tires and the rims are the chrome dimpled ones.

Interesting note: this number was set aside in 1963 and listed in the color consumer catalog as an International Truck Tractor, like the vibrator #1580. The realization at Aurora, that the tjet chassis had gears on top, meant that the articulated vibrator trailers #1585 and #1586 would never lash up without hitting the gears. The International was later modified into the tow truck #1364.

1362 Mack Dump Truck   1963-72
(CAB/BED)

- yellow/gray 3
- yellow/green 3
- turquoise/gray 2
- turquoise/green 2
- olive/gray 2
- red/gray 3
- red/green 3
- white/gray 3
- white/green 3
- green/gray 2
- tan/gray 3
- tan/green 3

The Mack Dump truck really says Ford on the front. The body style is that of the familiar cab over engine (COE) trucks that are still seen on the roads today. This truck is the same as the Vibrator #1582 in the previous chapter. The exception is that under the body the cutout prevalent in the vibrator version is not there. This is due to the more streamlined style of the tjet chassis. The body is 2 piece, a plate glued in the front under the cab holds in the glass. The bed is a separate piece and the front chrome is painted on. The trucks have never been found on the bubble pack.

1363 Mack Stake Truck   1963-72
(CAB/BED/STAKES)

- yellow/gray/gray 3
- yellow/gray/green 3
- yellow/green/green 3
- yellow/green/gray 3
- turquoise/gray/gray 1
- red/gray/gray 3
- red/gray/green 3
- tan/gray/gray 3
- tan/gray/green 3
- tan/green/green 3

Continued on next page.

1363 Mack Stake Truck   1963-72 (continued)
(CAB/BED/STAKES)

- white/green/green 3
- white/gray/green 3
- white/gray/gray 3
- white/green/gray 3
- olive/gray/gray 1
- green/gray/gray 2
- green/gray/green 2

Not shown:
- red/green/gray 3
- green/green/green 2
- turquoise/gray/green 1
- turquoise/green/gray 1
- olive/gray/green 1
- olive/green/gray 1
- red/gray/gray 3
- green/green/gray 2
- turquoise/green/green 1
- tan/green/gray 3
- olive/green/green 1

The Mack Stake truck really says Ford on the front. The body style is that of the familiar cab over engine (COE) trucks that are still seen on the roads today. This truck is the same as the Vibrator #1583 in the previous chapter. The exception is that under the body the cutout prevalent in the vibrator version is not there. This is due to the more streamlined style of the tjet chassis. The body is 2 piece, a plate glued in the front under the cab holds in the glass. The bed is a separate piece and the stakes are glued on all four sides. The front chrome is painted on. The trucks have never been found on the bubble pack.

1364 International Wrecker Tow Truck 1964-72
(BODY/SIDE STRIPE)

- yellow/red 3
- turquoise/black 0
- red/white/red top 0
- red/black 3
- tan/red 3
- white/red 3
- white/red/lemon bed 0
- green/black 2
- green/black olive bed 1
- olive/black 2

The tow truck started out as the Vibrator Semi #1580. When Aurora realized they could not have a semi like this as a tjet because of the chassis gears, they modified it into a tow truck. Great idea and a very popular truck in it's day. They removed the semi and trailers from the service manuals. The tow truck is a one piece molded body with a glued on top and an added bed in back with sides and inside detail. There is a boom painted black and NO tow hitch. The top is painted black and has a light instead of the familiar vibrator semi horn. Early versions of the tow truck will have a red top with a horn and different stripes on the sides of the bed. These are known as transition tow trucks and are not common. The front grille is sprayed on silver.

1365 (1265) Hot Rod Roadster 1964-72
(BODY/INTERIOR)

- yellow/red 3
- red/tan 3
- turquoise/black 2
- white/black 3
- white/red 3
- tan/black 3
- tan/red 3
- green/black 2
- olive/light green 2
- olive/black 2
- blue/black 2

Not shown:
- yellow/brown 3
- red/black 3
- tan/brown 3
- gray/black 0
- black/red 0

The Hot Rod started out as a Vibrator #1553. This car had three chrome pipes on each side and the doors were bubbled out to accommodate the wider thunderjet chassis. The roadster has a chrome windshield frame and chrome roll bar, along with a driver. There was a decal sheet packed in the box.

1366 (1266) Hot Rod Coupe 1964-72
(BODY-TOP/INTERIOR)

- yellow/red 3
- turquoise/black 3
- red/tan 3
- white/red 3
- white/black 3
- blue/black 2
- green/black 2
- tan/black 3
- tan/red 3
- tan/brown 3
- olive/light green 2
- gray/black 0
- black/red 0

The Hot Rod Coupe started out as a Vibrator car #1554. This car had three chrome pipes on each side and the doors were bubbled out to accommodate the wider thunderjet chassis. The coupe has a chrome windshield frame and a matching color top, with no driver. There was a decal sheet packed in the box.

1367 (1267) Maserati 1964-69
(BODY/STRIPE)

- yellow/red 4
- yellow 4
- red/white 4
- red 4
- blue/white 3
- white/red 4
- white 4
- turquoise/black 4
- turquoise 4
- green/white 3
- tan/black 4
- tan 4
- olive 2

Not Shown:
- blue 3
- green 3
- olive/white 2

Aurora's Maserati is often confused with the James Bond car, the Aston Martin DB4. It is a one piece molded body with separate chrome bumpers front and rear. They are very delicate and are often broken or missing. The rear bumper should have (3) vertical lights on each side and the front lights stick up. The "glass" is glued in place and the vent window posts are thin.

1368 (1268) Ferrari 250 GTO 1964-70
(BODY/STRIPES)

- yellow/red 4
- turquoise/black 3
- red/white 3
- red/black 1
- white/red 4
- blue/white 3
- green/white 1
- tan/black 4
- olive/white 3
- black/white (painted) 1

The Ferrari was a popular car. It is a one piece molded body with a rear bumper added on that is the same color as the car. The "glass" is glued in place and the front headlights are sprayed on. There are (2) stripes running front to back down the body.

1369 (1269) Classic Lincoln Continental 1964-69
(BODY)

- yellow 3
- turquoise 3
- red 3
- white 3
- tan 3

Continued on next page.

1369 (1269) Classic Lincoln Continental 1964-69 *(continued)*
(BODY)

The Lincoln always reminded me of Bruce Wayne's car that Alfred drove in the Batman TV show. I used it to go with my Batmobile #1385. The Lincoln is a one piece molded body with a very delicate chrome front bumper and a nice chrome continental kit rear bumper. The bumpers are always missing or broken which reduces the value significantly. The glass is glued in and molded in fender skirts cover half of the rear tires.

1370 (1270) A.C. COBRA 1964-69
(BODY/RUGS/SEATS)

- yellow/red/black 3
- yellow/brown/tan 3
- turquoise/black/gray 3
- turquoise/gray/black 3
- turquoise/black/red 3
- white/black/red 3
- white/red/black 3
- white/dark blue/light blue 1
- red/tan/black 3
- red/black/tan 3
- tan/brown/tan 3
- tan/black/red 3
- olive/gray/black 1

Not shown:
- yellow/brown/brown 3
- yellow/black/red
- red/black/gray 3
- tan/red/black 3
- tan/brown/red 3
- olive/lt green/blk 1
- black/red/blk (painted) 0

The AC Cobra has a rather "fat" appearance to it. It is a one piece molded body with delicate chrome plated bumperettes front and rear. They are often broken or missing as is with the convertible windshield and the drivers upper torso and head. The front screw post is in two different locations depending on which mold Aurora used. Probably a change necessitated by the Cigarbox or Speedline cars of the later sixties.

1371 (1271) '64 ½ Mustang Convertible 1964-69
(BODY/RUGS/SEATS/BOOT/STRIPES)

- yellow/black/dk red/black/red 3
- yellow/black/red/black/red 3
- yellow/brown/tan/brown 2
- yellow/red/black/black 3
- yellow/black/red/black 3
- turquoise/black/gray/black/black 3
- turquoise/gray/black/black 3
- red/tan/black/black 3
- red/black/tan/black 3
- green/black/gray/black/white 1
- tan/black/red/black/black 3
- tan/brown/tan/brown 2
- tan/red/black/black 3
- olive/black/lt green/black 1
- olive/black/lt green/olive 1

Continued on next page.

1371 (1271) '64 ½ Mustang Convertible 1964-69 (continued)
(BODY/RUGS/SEATS/BOOT/STRIPES)

Not shown:
- ☐ blue/black/gray/blk/wht 1
- ☐ black/red/blk/blk/wht 0

Many color combinations of pictured cars

- ☐ white/dk blue/lt blue/lt blue 1
- ☐ white/red/black/black/red 3
- ☐ white/red/black/red 2
- ☐ white/red/black/red 3

The Aurora Mustang was released the same day as Ford's 1:1 scale one. Aurora's racing contest featured the new Ford and Aurora was privy to the design drawings early on. Great car and a good seller. The body is one piece molded with separate front and rear chrome plated bumpers. The windshield and drivers torso were separate pieces and are often missing or broken. Many different color combinations exist.

1372 (1272) '64 ½ Mustang Hardtop 1964-69
(BODY/RUGS/SEATS/TOP/STRIPES)

- ☐ yellow/black/red/black/red 3
- ☐ yellow/brown/tan/yellow 2
- ☐ yellow/black/red/black 3
- ☐ yellow/red/black/black 3
- ☐ olive/black/lt green/light green 1
- ☐ red/tan/black/black 3
- ☐ red/tan/black/red 2
- ☐ red/black/tan/black 3
- ☐ red/black/tan/red 2
- ☐ white/black/red/black/black 3
- ☐ white/black/red/black 3
- ☐ white/red/black/black 3
- ☐ white/black/red/white 2
- ☐ white/dk blue/lt blue/white 1
- ☐ white/dk blue/lt blue/light blue 1
- ☐ tan/black/red/black/black 3
- ☐ tan/red/black/black 3
- ☐ tan/black/red/tan/black 2
- ☐ tan/red/black/tan 2
- ☐ tan/brown/tan/brown 2

Not shown:
- ☐ green/black/gray/green/white 1
- ☐ blue/black/gray/black/white 1
- ☐ black/red/black/white (painted) 0

Many other color combinations exist.

- ☐ turquoise/black/gray/black/black 3
- ☐ turquoise/black/gray/turquoise 2
- ☐ turquoise/gray/black/turquoise 2

The Aurora Mustang was released the same day as Ford's 1:1 scale one. Aurora's racing contest featured the new Ford and Aurora was privy to the design drawings early on. Great car and a good seller. The body is one piece molded with separate front and rear chrome plated bumpers. The top is one piece and painted on the inside. Combinations where the top and body are the same color are more desirable. Many different color combinations are known to exist.

1373 (1273) '64 ½ Mustang Fastback 2+2 1966-70
(BODY/RUGS/SEATS/STRIPES)

- yellow/black/red/red 3
- yellow/black/red/black 3
- turquoise/black/gray/black 3
- red/black/tan/white 3
- red/tan/black/white 3
- white/black/red/black 3
- tan/black/red/black 3
- blue/black/gray/white 1
- green/black/gray/white 1
- olive/black/gray/white 1
- black/red/black/white 0
- candy red/black/black/silver 0
- candy green/black/black/silver 0
- candy blue/black/black/silver 0

Aurora's racing contest, The Ford-Aurora Grand Nationals, featured the Ford Fastback in 1965. Great car and a good seller. The body is one piece molded with separate front and rear chrome plated bumpers. It is the same as the convertible and hardtop. The top is one piece and painted on the inside. The top and body always had stripes on the production models. The Candy red, green, and blue are the toughest to get and were only offered in a Competition Pac. Different interior combinations are likely to exist. Rarity would be based on the solid colors.

1374 (1274) Ford GT 1966-72
(BODY/STRIPE)

- turquoise/black 5
- red/black 5
- red/white 3
- white/red 3
- white/wide black 4
- white/black 5
- medium blue/black 5
- blue/white 4
- green/white 3
- olive/white 3

Not shown:
- white/blue stripe 2
- olive/black 3

- tan/black 5
- black (molded)/white 2

The Ford GT was probably the most popular of the Tjets. There were literally millions made and the car is an excellent body for racing. It is a one piece molded body with full glass inside. The headlights are detailed in chrome paint and there is a stripe down the center along with side stripes. The top stripe can be narrow on older cars and wider on later manufactured versions.

1375 (1275) Cobra GT 1966-72
(BODY/STRIPES)

- yellow/black 5
- turquoise/black 5
- red/white 5
- white/blue 3
- white/black 5
- blue/white 3
- green/white 3
- olive/white 3
- tan/black 5
- black (painted)/white 1

Not Shown: white/red 3   olive/black 3

The Cobra GT is a one piece molded body with full "glass". The headlights are painted silver and the car always has (2) stripes.

1376 (1276) Porsche 904 1966-70
(BODY/STRIPE)

- yellow/red 5
- turquoise/black 5
- red/white 5
- white/red 5
- blue/white 3
- tan/black 5
- green/white 3
- olive/white 3
- black (painted)/white 1

Aurora's paperwork all says this car is a Porsche 906, but it is actually a 904. It is a one piece molded body with full "glass". There is a single stripe and the headlights are painted silver.

1377 (1277) Chaparral 1966-72
(BODY/NUMBER)

- yellow #2 5
- yellow #3 5
- yellow #3 w/roll bar 4
- yellow #5 5
- yellow #7 5
- red #2 w/roll bar 4
- red #3 5
- red #5 5
- red #7 5
- red #7 w/roll bar 4

Continued on next page.

1377 (1277) Chaparral 1966-72 (continued)
(BODY/NUMBER)

☐ turquoise #2 5	☐ turquoise #3 5	☐ turquoise #5 5	☐ turquoise #7 5	☐ black (painted) #7 1
☐ white #2 5	☐ white #5 5	☐ white #7 5	☐ blue #3 3	☐ blue #7 3
☐ green/#2 3	☐ green #3 3	☐ green #7 3	☐ olive #2 w/roll bar 2	☐ olive #5 3
☐ tan #2 5	☐ tan #5 w/roll bar 4	☐ tan #7 5		

Not shown: Many different color and number combinations exist, with or without the roll bar.

When Aurora was designing this car they had limited photos of the real thing to work on and the perspectives were off a bit. The car came out too narrow and really did not look as proportionate as it should have to the Jim Hall Chaparral it was modeled after. The car is a one piece molded body with a fitted windshield on it. There are 16 chrome pipes behind the driver in an 4-8-4 arrangement. They are commonly broken. The early production cars had a chrome squared off roll bar behind the driver and it is often missing. Later versions plugged the holes and eliminated it all together, probably to reduce cost and customer complaints. There is a number on the hood of the car.

1378 (1278) Lola GT 1966-70
(BODY/STRIPE)

☐ yellow/red 5	☐ yellow/black 4	☐ yellow/black-white 4	☐ olive/silver/black 3	☐ green/white 3
☐ turquoise/black 5	☐ turquoise/wht-blk 4	☐ turquoise/blk-wht 4	☐ white/red-blk 4	☐ white/red 5

The Lola GT is a one piece molded body with a full glass. Some of these cars have a double stripe down the center and there are different color combinations to the stripe. Others have a single stripe down the center. There is also a side stripe along with silver painted headlights.

Continued on next page.

1378 (1278) Lola GT 1966-70 (continued)
(BODY/STRIPE)

- red/white-black 4
- red/white 5
- red/silver-black 4
- tan/white-black 4
- black(painted)/wht-red 1
- blue/white 3
- (2) piece clamshell box with label

Not shown:
- white/black 4
- turquoise/white-red 4

Many other stripe combinations exist.

The Lola GT is a one piece molded body with a full "glass". Some of these cars have a double stripe down the center and there are different color combinations to the stripe. Others have a single stripe down the center. There is also a side stripe along with silver painted headlights.

1379 (1279) Toronado 1966-70
(BODY)

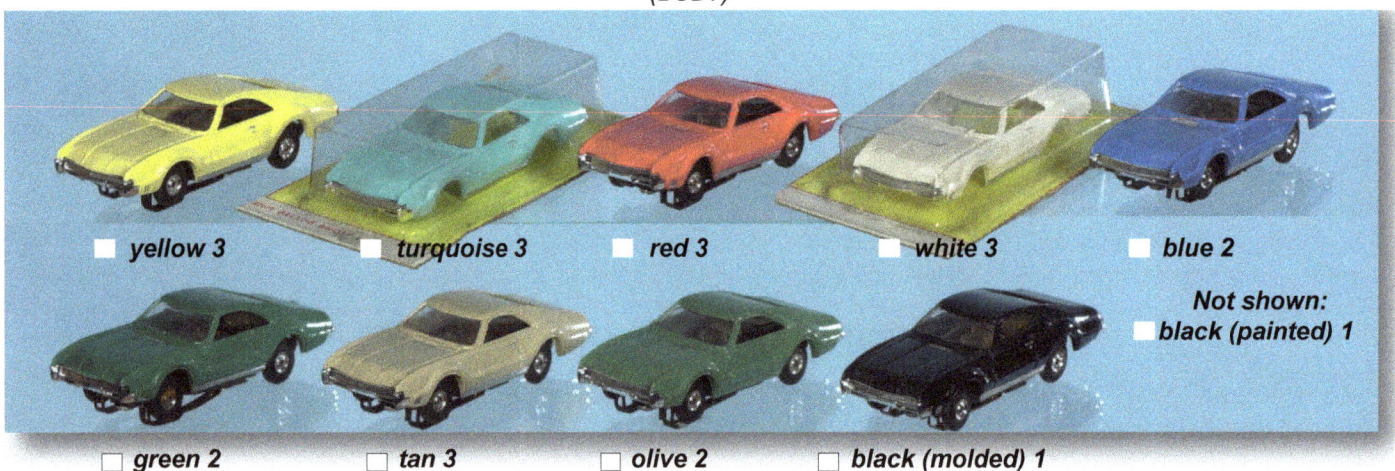

- yellow 3
- turquoise 3
- red 3
- white 3
- blue 2
- green 2
- tan 3
- olive 2
- black (molded) 1

Not shown:
- black (painted) 1

The Toronado was an interesting choice to be modeled by Aurora. One of the company's owners had one and suggested they do it. The body is a one piece molded one with a full "glass". The bumpers are separate chrome plated ones. Appearance wise the hood seems too long for the body.

1380 (1280) Mako Shark 1966-72
(BODY)

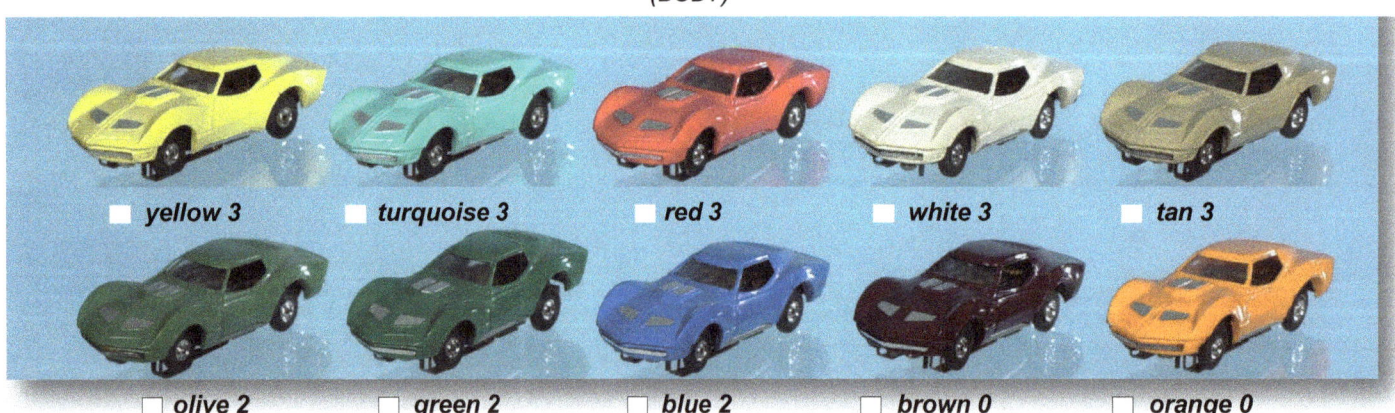

- yellow 3
- turquoise 3
- red 3
- white 3
- tan 3
- olive 2
- green 2
- blue 2
- brown 0
- orange 0

Continued on next page.

1380 (1280) Mako Shark 1966-72 *(continued)*

The Mako Shark is modeled after the Corvette show car. Aurora's is a one piece molded body with a small windshield and very fragile front window posts. They are almost always bent or broken on used cars. The front and rear bumpers are chrome plated separate pieces. When the body was modified for Speedline cars in the later '60's, Aurora enlarged the wheel wells to allow for the bigger push car wheels. The light orange and brown colors are always with the larger wheel wells.

1381 (1281) Dino Ferrari 1966-72
(BODY/STRIPE)

- ☐ yellow/red 5
- ☐ turquoise/black 5
- ☐ red/white 5
- ☐ white/red 5
- ☐ tan/black 5
- ☐ olive/white 3
- ☐ green/white 4
- ☐ blue/white 4

Not shown:
- ☐ black/white (painted) 1

The Dino Ferrari is a one piece molded body with a full "glass" with a large rear deck displaying the gears of the chassis. The headlights are paiinted silver and there is a stripe down the center of the car.

1382 (1282) Ford J Car 1966-72
(BODY/HOOD)

- ☐ yellow/black 5
- ☐ turquoise/black 5
- ☐ red/black 5
- ☐ green/black 4
- ☐ blue/black 4
- ☐ white/blue 5
- ☐ white/black 3
- ☐ white/butterscotch 1
- ☐ tan/brown 4
- ☐ black/white (molded) 2

Not shown: ☐ olive/black 3

The Ford J Car is a one piece molded body with a small windshield "glass". The front of the car is mask sprayed and the side stripes match. The headlights are painted silver. This was a very popular car of the day and they are quite common today.

1383 (1283) '67 Thunderbird 1966-69
(BODY)

- ☐ yellow 4
- ☐ turquoise 4
- ☐ red 4
- ☐ white 4
- ☐ tan 4

Continued on next page.

1383 (1283) '67 Thunderbird 1966-69 (continued)
(BODY)

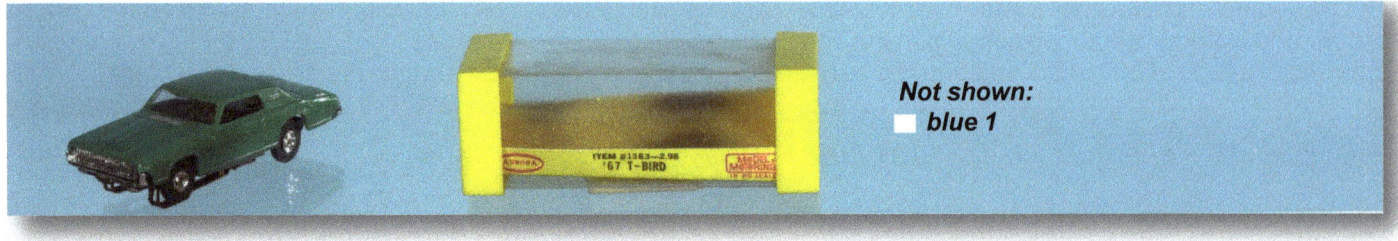

☐ green 3   typical box with insert

Not shown:
☐ blue 1

The '67 Ford Thunderbird was introduced to coincide with the 1966 Ford Aurora Grand Nationals races. (*See* chapter 5) This car is a one piece molded body with full "glass". It has chrome plated bumpers front and rear. The hood appears to be out of proportion to the rest of the car.

The chrome plated version was offered as the in-store championship prize for the 1966 Ford-Aurora Grand Nationals. It is highly desirable today. It is frequently mistaken as the plated Speedline car which usually has a shortened front screw post.

1384 (1284) Green Hornet's Black Beauty 1967-69
(BODY/STICKER)
1385 (1285) Batmobile 1967-70
(BODY)

☐ Holland box   typical box with insert   ☐ Green Hornet 2   ☐ Batmobile 2

The Black Beauty is a faithful replica of the real car. The body is one piece and the windshield posts are very fragile and are often bent or broken. The windshield "glass" fits poorly in the front and allows the top to be squeezed down thus bending the vent window posts. The chassis is a tight fit against the fender skirts causing most used examples to have cut rear wheel wells for clearance. The Hornet sticker on the top is paper and should be present on a new mint car. Nice chrome mask sprayed accents show off the grill and headlights. Bumpers are molded in.

The Batmobile is a very detailed replica of the real thing, right down to the (3) stacks behind the heads of Batman and Robin. It is a one piece molded body with molded in bumpers and a (2) piece "glass" canopy. Red trim and red bat insignias on the doors accent the car.

1386 (1286) '67 Ford Galaxie XL500 1967-70
(BODY)

☐ yellow 4   ☐ turquoise 4   ☐ red 4   ☐ white 4   ☐ blue 3

☐ green 3   ☐ tan 4   ☐ chrome (promo) 1

not shown:
☐ black (molded) 1

Continued on next page.

1386 (1286) '67 Ford Galaxie XL500 1967-70 *(continued)*

The XL500 is a one piece molded body with full windshield glass. There are separate front and rear chrome plated bumpers. The rear wheel openings are rounded off and appear to be cut on a car right out of the mold. This is not the case. There are mask sprayed accents to finish off a clean sleek look to the car.

1387 (1287) Thunderbike 1967-70
(BIKE/DRIVER)

☐ red-ylw/ylw-blk 3   ☐ red-slv/red-blk 3   ☐ red-blk/red-blk 3   ☐ red-blk/wht-blk 3   ☐ blu-slv/blu-blk 3

Not shown: ☐ red-wht/wht-blk 3   ☐ red-blk/yle-blk 3
             ☐ blu-blk/blu-blk 3   ☐ wine-blk-slv/wine-blk 2

☐ body, bar, gas tank, fender kit 3

The Aurora Thunderbike was a great idea but unfortunately it ran terribly. You could not make a turn without the bike tipping over. It was clearly out of scale to HO. The chassis was a modified thunderjet one turned vertical. The driver is a separate molded piece as were the gas tank and the front headlight. The bike came in a variety of color combinations and is a popular item today.

1388 (1288) Camaro 1967-70
(BODY/STRIPE)

☐ yellow/black 4   ☐ turquoise/black 4   ☐ red/black 4   ☐ white/black 4   ☐ blue/black 3

☐ blue/white 3   ☐ green/black   ☐ tan/black 4   ☐ lime/green   ☐ brown/gold 1

not shown: ☐ green/white 3

☐ black/white 2

Aurora's Camaro was a popular car with a history of production problems. The body is one piece molded with a glass windshield and chrome plated bumpers front and rear. There is a stripe across the hood and mask sprayed detail on the sides. The mold was damaged and the sides of the Firebird mold were used. Some later models have different rocker panels than the first production cars. The name CAMARO molded in the side can be large or small print. The rear wheel well openings were made larger to accommodate the Speedline tires and this carried over to the later colors like lime green and brown. The front chrome grill has (2) versions to fit the Speedline chassis also.

1389 (1289) Cougar 1967-70
(BODY)

☐ yellow 4   ☐ turquoise 4   ☐ red 4   ☐ white 4   ☐ blue 3
☐ green 3   ☐ tan 4   ☐ black (molded) 1

Aurora's Cougar was a good replica of the real car. The body is one piece molded with a glass windshield and chrome plated bumpers front and rear. There is mask sprayed detail on the sides.

1391 (1291) Candy '63 Corvette 1966-69
(BODY)

☐ painted red 2   ☐ painted blue 2   ☐ painted green 2

not shown:
☐ plated red 4
☐ plated green 4
☐ plated peach 4

☐ plated blue 4   ☐ plated copper 4   ☐ plated purple 4

This was the first in a series of Thunderjets called the candy cars. The '60's featured many candy colored real cars in metalflake and Aurora used a marketing strategy to capitalize on a fad of the day. They "candy" painted existing Tjets (*see* #1356) to give them more appeal to the kids. Today the candy painted ones are the more desirable for (2) reasons. They came out first and the paint has a tendency to wear off from handling. The later version plated ones were metallized after Aurora perfected the vacuum metallizing process. These were more durable but could be chipped.

1392 (1292) Candy XKE Jaguar 1966-69

☐ painted red 2   ☐ painted blue 2   ☐ painted green 2

not shown:
☐ plated red 4

☐ plated blue 4   ☐ plated peach 4   ☐ plated green 2   ☐ plated purple 4   ☐ plated copper 4

Continued on next page.

1392 (1292) Candy XKE Jaguar 1966-69 *(continued)*

They candy painted existing Tjets (*see* #1358) to give them more appeal to the kids. Today the candy painted ones are the more desirable for (2) reasons. They came out first and the paint has a tendency to wear off from handling. The later version plated ones were metallized after Aurora perfected the vacuum metallizing process. These were more durable but could be chipped.

1393 (1293) Candy Gran Prix Racer 1966-69

- painted red 2
- painted blue 2
- painted green 2

not shown:
- plated green 4
- plated peach 4
- plated purple 4

- plated blue 4
- plated red 4
- plated copper 4

They candy painted existing Tjets (*see* #1361) to give them more appeal to the kids. Today the candy painted ones are the more desirable for (2) reasons. They came out first and the paint has a tendency to wear off from handling. The later version plated ones were metallized after Aurora perfected the vacuum metallizing process. These were more durable but could be chipped.

1394 (1294) Candy Ferrari 1966-69
(BODY)

- painted red 2
- painted blue 2
- painted green 2

not shown:
- plated blue 4
- plated red 4
- plated peach 4

- plated purple 4
- plated copper 4
- plated green 4

They candy painted existing Tjets (*see* #1368) to give them more appeal to the kids. Today the candy painted ones are the more desirable for (2) reasons. They came out first and the paint has a tendency to wear off from handling. The later version plated ones were metallized after Aurora perfected the vacuum metallizing process. These were more durable but could be chipped.

1395 (1295) Candy Ford GT 1966-69
(BODY)

- painted red 2
- painted blue 2
- painted green 2
- plated purple 4
- plated peach 4

Not shown:
- plated red 4
- plated blue 4
- plated green 4
- plated copper 4

Continued on next page.

1395 (1295) Candy Ford GT 1966-69 *(continued)*

They candy painted existing Tjets (*see* #1374) to give them more appeal to the kids. Today the candy painted ones are the more desirable for (2) reasons. They came out first and the paint has a tendency to wear off from handling. The later version plated ones were metallized after Aurora perfected the vacuum metallizing process. These were more durable but could be chipped.

1396 (1296) Candy Cobra GT 1966-69
(BODY)

- painted red 2
- painted blue 2
- painted green 2
- plated copper 4
- plated purple 4
- plated peach 4

not shown:
- plated blue 4
- plated red 4
- plated green 4

They candy painted existing Tjets (*see* #1375) to give them more appeal to the kids. Today the candy painted ones are the more desirable for (2) reasons. They came out first and the paint has a tendency to wear off from handling. The later version plated ones were metallized after Aurora perfected the vacuum metallizing process. These were more durable but could be chipped.

1397 (1297) McLaren Elva 1968-72
(BODY/STRIPES)

- yellow/red 4
- turquoise/white 4
- red/white 4
- white/red 4
- blue/white 3
- green/white 3
- tan/white 2

The McLaren is a one piece molded body with mask sprayed headlights and a stripe down the center. There are (8) chrome exhaust stacks behind the driver and a simulated spare tire under the cockpit windshield. The car is seldom found with the wheel wells cut as it has ample openings for larger tires.

1398 (1299) Dune Buggy Roadster 1969-72
(BODY)

- yellow/roll bar 2
- yellow 4
- turquoise 4
- red 4
- white 4

Continued on next page.

1398 (1298) Dune Buggy Roadster 1969-72 (continued)
(BODY)

☐ green 3   ☐ blue 3

Picture the late '60's and you have to think of a Dune Buggy. Sand, surf, and all the rest. Aurora's Dune Buggy Roadster had a very fragile windshield and a driver inside. Both are commonly missing on used examples. There is a mask sprayed spare in the back and silver headlights. The tires are usually the oversize knobby sidewall type with the chromed or yellow (3) dimple hubs.

1399 (1299) Dune Buggy Coupe 1969-72
(BODY)

☐ yellow 4   ☐ turquoise 4   ☐ white 4   ☐ red 4   ☐ blue 3

☐ purple 1   ☐ green 3   ☐ orange 1   ☐ medium blue 3   ☐ lime 1

Picture the late '60's and you have to think of a Dune Buggy. Sand, surf, and all the rest. Aurora's Dune Buggy Coupe had a stronger attachment to the windshield as it was glued to the canopy roof. There is no driver inside. There is a mask sprayed spare in the back and silver headlights. The tires are usually the oversize knobby sidewall type with the chromed or yellow (3) dimple hubs.

1400 (1100) Mangusta 1969-72
(BODY)

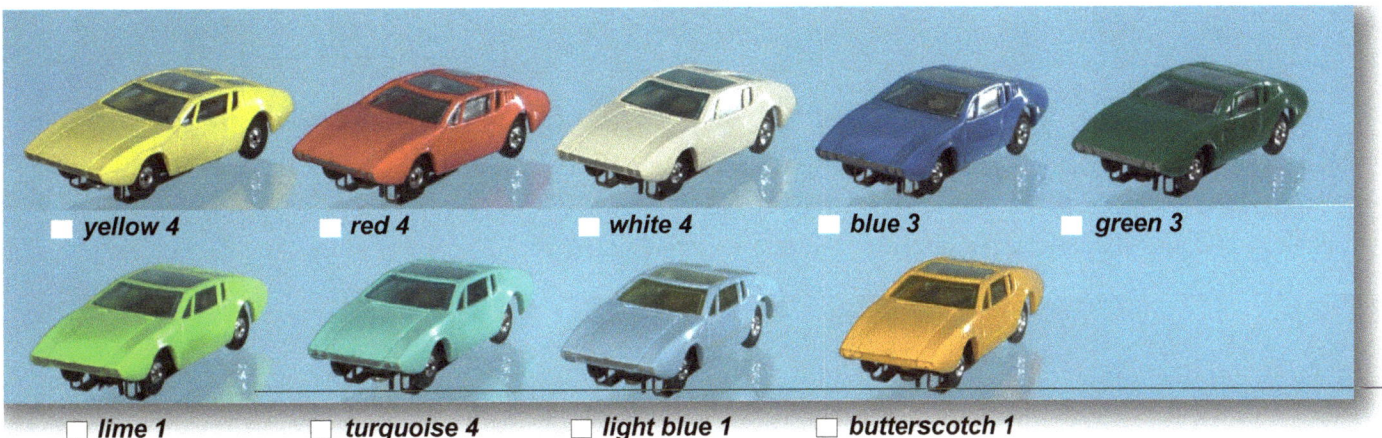

☐ yellow 4   ☐ red 4   ☐ white 4   ☐ blue 3   ☐ green 3

☐ lime 1   ☐ turquoise 4   ☐ light blue 1   ☐ butterscotch 1

The Mangusta is a one piece molded body with molded in front and rear bumpers. The windshield "glass" is very large and is tinted green.

1401 (1101) WILLY'S "GASSER" 1969-72
(BODY)

☐ yellow 3   ☐ red 3   ☐ green 2

not shown:
several different colors that are Cigarbox or Speedline cars. These shown are the basic Thunderjet colors.

☐ white 3   ☐ bright white 3   ☐ blue 2

The Willys is one of the most popular of the Tjets. It is frequently copied today and one must be careful of fakes in the rarer colors. The Willys is a one piece molded body with a molded in rear nerf bar. The headlights, blower cover, and tail lights are mask sprayed. There is full "glass" inside. A set of decals comes inside the box along with the car. Many of the Cigarbox and Speedline, and Speedster versions are passed off as original tjets. The front post is a sure giveaway as the tjet is longer.

1402 (1102) Pontiac Firebird 1969-72
(BODY)

☐ yellow 4   ☐ red 4   ☐ white   ☐ blue 3   ☐ green 3

The Aurora Firebird is a one piece molded body with front and rear chrome separate bumpers. There is a full windshield. Side cams that were used in the mold were shared with some of the #1388 Camaro's.

1403 (1103) Cheetah 1969-72
(BODY)

☐ yellow 4   ☐ red 4   ☐ white 4   ☐ blue 3   ☐ green 3

The Cheetah is a one piece molded body with no bumpers. There are mask sprayed headlights and accents. The car is short and just fits under a tjet chassis. There is a windshield "glass".

1404 (1104) Volkswagen 1969-72
(BODY/FLOWERS)

☐ lemon/round 1 ☐ yellow/pointed 4 ☐ yellow/round 4 ☐ snow white/round 1 ☐ white/round 4

☐ blue/pointed 3 ☐ blue/round 3 ☐ green pointed 3 ☐ red/pointed 4 ☐ red/round 4

Aurora's Volkswagen idea was actually "borrowed" from the German slot car company, Faller. Faller made mostly German cars and their Volkswagen was very thin plastic. Aurora made some subtle changes such as thickening the plastic and also adding mask sprayed flowers to it to give that "hippy" look of the '60's. The front and rear chrome bumpers are separate pieces and they were held on by the unusually long chassis screws that aurora used on this car. That was the only time they deviated in chassis mounting screw length. The bumpers are commonly missing on used Volkswagens.

1405 (1105) McLaren BRM Formula 1 1969-72
1406 (1106) Repco Brabham Formula 1 1969-72
(BODY/NUMBER)

box with insert ☐ red#11 4 **box with insert** ☐ green #2 4

Aurora made their first major chassis change to allow for the narrow Formula 1 body to fit. The Slimline chassis was designed and it used different parts such as magnets, brushes, and a smaller armature to name a few. The McLaren BRM was only offered in one color and it had a helmeted drivers head in addition to a chrome plated rollbar and engine. The rear exhaust was a separate chrome plated piece that was held on by the rear screw. The hole in it was too small after plating and it always broke when attached. Most are missing from used examples. The Repco Brabham was only offered in one color and it had a helmeted drivers head in addition to a chrome plated engine. The sides have a separate gray plastic piece on each simulatiing the rear suspension.

1407 (1107) Dodge Charger 1969-72
(BODY/STRIPES)

☐ lemon/black 2 ☐ yellow/black 4 ☐ turquoise/black 3 ☐ red/black 4 ☐ blue/black 3

Continued on next page.

43

1407 (1107) Dodge Charger 1969-72 (continued)
(BODY/STRIPES)

- ☐ snow white/black 2
- ☐ snow white/red 2
- ☐ white/black 4
- ☐ purple/black 1
- ☐ purple/white 1
- ☐ green/black 3
- ☐ lime/black 3
- ☐ light green/black 1
- ☐ orange/black 1

not shown:
- ☐ olive drab/black 1

The Charger is a favorite muscle car among collectors. The car is a one piece molded body with separate chrome plated bumpers front and rear. There is a full windshield "glass" and fragile side window vent posts that are easily bent or broken. The black top is mask sprayed on along with (2) stripes running side to side on the trunk lid.

1408 (1108) Ford Torino 1969-72
(BODY/STRIPES)

- ☐ yellow/black 3
- ☐ red/white 3
- ☐ white/red 3

not shown:
- ☐ black/white 1

- ☐ green/white 3
- ☐ green/gold 2
- ☐ black/gold 1

The Ford Torino is another popular '60's muscle car. This was a one piece molded body and the front and rear chrome plated bumpers are separate pieces. There are mask sprayed stripes down the sides of the car that are commonly worn off from handling.

1409 (1109) Alfa Romeo 1970-72
(BODY/ROLLBAR)

- ☐ yellow/yellow 4
- ☐ yellow/chrome 4
- ☐ yellow/(white ball) 3
- ☐ red/red 4
- ☐ red/chrome 4
- ☐ white/chrome 4
- ☐ blue/blue 3
- ☐ blue/chrome 3
- ☐ green/green 3
- ☐ green/chrome 3

Continued on next page.

1409 (1109) Alfa Romeo 1970-72 (continued)
(BODY/ROLLBAR)

The Alfa Romeo is a one piece body with molded in front and rear bumpers. There is a cockpit "glass" and there are either a chrome plated roll bar or a roll bar the color of the car. The #31 on the sides is in (2) different sizes, and the drivers head can be helmeted or not. Most cars have been seen any combination of variations and rarity does not appear to be affected.

1410 (1110) Chaparral 2F 1970-72
(BODY)

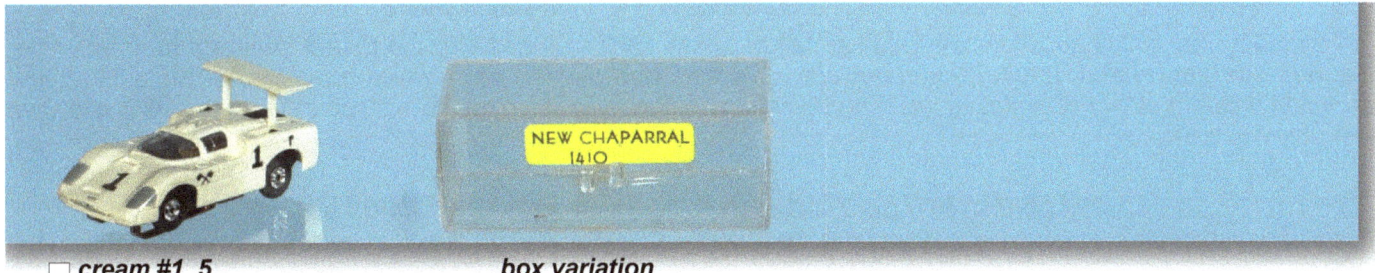

☐ cream #1 5   box variation

The Chaparral 2F has the #1 mask sprayed on it. There is a separate wing attached to the car. This is always missing and affects the rarity. There is a windshield "glass".

1411 (1111) GTO Convertible 1971-72
(BODY/TOP)

☐ butterscotch 1   ☐ red 3   ☐ white 2   ☐ snow white 3   ☐ medium blue 2

☐ brown w/silver stripes 0   ☐ brown/black top 4   ☐ brown 4

The GTO convertible actually has the top up but is a rippled top like that of a convertible. Interesting concept and I am not sure of the reason for it. There is a chrome plated separate piece bumper front and rear. The rear bumper falls off easily while the front one is protected and more secure. There is a mask sprayed silver stripe around the wheel wells and they are often found cut.

1414 (1114) AMX 1970-72
(BODY/STRIPES)

☐ lemon/black 3   ☐ white/red 4   ☐ orange/mustard 2   ☐ medium blue/white 3   ☐ lime/black 2

The AMX is a very good job of scale with plenty of detail molded in. There are separate chrome bumpers front and rear as well as a full windshield "glass". There are (2) stripes mask sprayed down the center of the car.

1415 (1115) Mach 1 Mustang 1970-72
(BODY)

☐ yellow 3   ☐ white 3   ☐ red 2   ☐ medium blue 2   ☐ blue 3

The Mustang Mach 1 is a good scale representation of the 1:1 car. It has chrome plated separate bumpers front and rear. The windshield glass is full abd has a side vent window molded into it which accounts for the fact that few are found with broken vent window posts. The hood is mask sprayed flat black as well as side stripes. This is a very desirable car today.

1416 (1116) The Wild Mustang Fastback 2+2 1969-70
1417 (1117) The Wild Ford GT 1969-70
1418 (1118) The Wild Camaro 1969-70
1419 (1119) The Wild Cougar 1969-70
(BODY/STRIPES/NUMBER)

☐ white/red 3   ☐ white/orange 4   ☐ white/blue 3   ☐ white/red 3   typical box with insert

The Wild Ones were introduced in 1969 as the fastest, hottest, Model Motoring Screamers ever made. They were (4) previously manufactured body styles with newer appointments. They had hot armatures, silver plated pickups, silver plated brushes, spongee slicks, competition stripes and numbers, and a decal sheet. The Mustang is the same body as #1373. The Ford GT is the same body as #1374. The Camaro is the same body as #1388. The Cougar is the same body as #1389

1421 (1121) '32 Ford Pick Up Truck 1970-72
(BODY)

☐ lemon 3   ☐ red 2   ☐ orange 2   ☐ lime 2   ☐ medium blue 2

Aurora is said to have taken some liberties with the "Mini Lindy" version of this truck made by Lindberg. The '32 Ford is a narrow body and is the only other thunderjet that makes use of the slimline chassis used for the Formula 1 cars. There is a chrome plated engine and headlights attached to the front. The seat and windshield "glass" are separate pieces. There is a small license plate molded in the rear below the tailgate and the bed is mask sprayed black.

1429 (1129) El Camino Pick Up Truck 1970-72
(BODY/SURF BOARDS/TOP)

☐ yellow/white (blk top) 2 ☐ yellow 4 ☐ turquoise (shade) 3 ☐ turquoise 3 ☐ red 3

☐ white 3 ☐ white 3 ☐ blue 1

The El Camino is a one piece molded body with separate chrome plated bumpers front and rear. There is a full windshield "glass" and the bed in back is mask sprayed black. So far, only the yellow version has been reported as having a black mask sprayed top in addition to an unpainted top. All others are unpainted. The surfboards are attached by heat staking from underneath. There is a design on the boards and the board color is never the same as the car. There can be different colored boards on different cars, but those shown are the most common.

1430 (1130) Ford J Car "Flamethrower" 1970-72
1431 (1131) McLaren Elva "Flamethrower" 1970-72
(BODY/TOP)

☐ white/blue 5 ☐ black/white 5 ☐ green/white 2 ☐ red/white 3

Aurora introduced the "Flamethrowers" as cars with headlights and tail lights. There was a small light bulb on the chassis and clear plastic to transmit the light. Great idea but the car's performance suffered for the drain of power. The Ford J Car is identical to the #1382. The lighted one was only available in one color combination. The McLaren Elva is identical to the #1397 and was available in the combinations shown above.

TUFF ONES

Aurora needed to introduce a new breed of thunderjet to compete with the latest releases from the competition. They introduced Tuff Ones. These cars were speed timed and track tested at 760 MPH. They sported a new rewound and tested armature, extra power oriented magnets, Mag style wheels, high silver content brushes, independent front wheels, super wide sponge tires, and non-snag silver pick up shoes. The cars were existing bodies with newer, more modern paint jobs and colors. Aurora released a set of six cars and then released another six as a follow on.

1471 (1171) Lola GT "Tuff Ones" 1970-72
1472 (1172) Ford GT "Tuff Ones" 1970-72
(BODY/STRIPE)

☐ lemon/pink 4 ☐ black/pink 5 ☐ light blue/orange 4 ☐ light blue/orange (diff. #5) 4

The Lola GT is the same body as #1378. The paint scheme and #3 is new. There was a 2 for 1 special Aurora offered where the body came unfinished on a piece of track as a free offer (*see* page 54). The Ford GT is the same as #1374 with a newer paint scheme and #5. There was a 2 for 1 special Aurora offered where the body came unfinished on a piece of track as a free offer (*see* page 54).

1473 (1173) Dune Buggy Coupe "Tuff Ones" 1970-72
(BODY/TOP)
1474 (1174) Willys Gasser "Tuff Ones" 1970-72
(BODY/STRIPES)
1475 (1175) Cheetah "Tuff Ones" 1970-72

☐ lemon/blue-white 4 ☐ lemon/purple 3 ☐ lemon light purple 3 ☐ orange 4

The Dune Buggy Coupe is the same body as #1399. The color is new. There was a 2 for 1 special Aurora offered where the body came unfinished on a piece of track as a free offer with no top (*see* page 54). The Willys Gasser is the same body as #1401. The paint scheme is new. There was a 2 for 1 special Aurora offered where the body came unfinished on a piece of track as a free offer (*see* page 54). The Cheetah is the same body as #1403. The paint scheme and #2 is new. There was a 2 for 1 special Aurora offered where the body came unfinished on a piece of track as a free offer (*see* page 54).

1476 (1176) Chaparral 2F "Tuff Ones" 1970-72
(BODY)

☐ lime/blue 2   ☐ snow wht/blk 4   ☐ snow wht/blu/slv trm 3   ☐ snow wht/blu 4   ☐ white/blue 4

The Chaparral 2F is the same body as #1410. The paint scheme and #10 is new. There was a 2 for 1 special Aurora offered where the body came unfinished on a piece of track as a free offer (*see* page 54).

1477 (1177) AMX "Tuff Ones" 1971-72
(BODY)

☐ red/white/blue 3   ☐ red/silver (painted bumpers) 5   ☐ white/blue 5

The AMX Tuff Ones is the same car as #1414. The paint scheme is different.

1478 (1178) Firebird "Tuff Ones" 1971-72
(BODY/HOOD/NUMBER)

☐ lemon/black/#7 4   ☐ yellow/black/#7 2   ☐ yellow/black 2   ☐ snow wht/red/#7 1   ☐ snow white 3

The Firebird Tuff Ones is the same body as the #1402 Firebird. The paint scheme is different.

1479 (1179) Cougar "Tuff Ones" 1971-72
(BODY/SIDES/NUMBER)
1480 (1180) Camaro "Tuff Ones" 1971-72
1481 (1181) Dino Ferrari "Tuff Ones" 1971-72
1482 (1182) Volkswagen "Tuff Ones" 1971-72
(BODY/STRIPE/NUMBER)

☐ white/butterscotch/#21   ☐ blue/yellow/#1   ☐ red/white-green/#3   ☐ orange/black-white/#2

The Cougar Tuff Ones is the same body style as the #1389 Cougar with a new paint scheme. The Camaro Tuff Ones is the same body style as #11388 with a new paint scheme. The catalog shows the car with the #4 on it and the production version had the #1. The Tuff Ones Dino Ferari is the same as #1381 with a new updated paint scheme and a colored windshield. The Volkswagen Tuff Ones is the same as #1404 with a newer updated paint scheme and colored windshield glass.

1483 (1183) Sand Van Dune Buggy 1971-72
(BODY/TOP)

☐ *pink/white 4* ☐ *lime/white 4* ☐ *medium blue/white 1* ☐ *orange/white 1*

The Sand Van Dune Buggy is California styled with cathedral rear windows and a two tone top. Superfat sponge tires were stock items. The body is that of the Dune Buggy #1398/#1399.

1484 (1184) Super Modified Roadster 1971-72
(BODY)

☐ *lemon 3* ☐ *orange 3* ☐ *blue3*

The Super Modified is the body of #1365/1366 with different colors and a set of mounting holes up each side for the side nerf bars. There are chrome seperate piece nerf bars front and rear. They are held on by the body screws. The side nerf bar/pipes are chrome pieces and the top wing and roll cage is chrome also. All of these extra parts are often broken or missing from the car. There are superfat sponge tires on the rear.

1485 (1185) Snowmobile 1971-72
(BODY/DRIVER)

☐ **butterscotch/blue 3** ☐ **blue/lemon 3** *typical box with end-cap label*

The Snowmobile was made as a toy to use up the extra thunderjet chassis that were over ordered by Aurora's purchasing department. The body and driver are way out of scale to the HO cars and are close to the #1387 Thunderbike. This vehicle has separate skis on the front and a chrome blower and motor. The driver and snowmobiles come in different color combinations.

1487 Good Humor Truck 1972
(BODY/DECALS)

☐ **white/wild huckleberry decals 3**

The Good Humor Truck is a good scale replica of the real thing. The front bumper is chrome plated and there is a Good Humor Man inside the cab. There is a windshield. There is a decal sheet and instructions that come with the truck. The Wild Huckleberry decals go across the sides and the popsicle goes on the door. These are frequently missing and do affect the value. There are some trucks that were packaged in mailers and given out to the Good Humor Company.

1491 (1191) Chaparral 2F "Flamethrower" 1971-72
(BODY/BODY/NUMBER)
1493 (1193) Ferrari "Flamethrower" 1971-72
(BODY/STRIPES)

☐ snow white/#1 5   ☐ medium blue/white 4   ☐ red/white 2

The Chaparral 2F is the same body style as #1410 thunderjet except this one has the holes for the flamethrower option. There is also a different paint scheme. The Ferrari is the same body style as #1368 with the flamethrower modifications added.

1494 (1194) Ford GT "Flamethrower" 1971-72
(BODY/STRIPE)
1495 (1195) Cobra GT "Flamethrower" 1971-72
(BODY/STRIPES)

not shown:
☐ brown/white 2

☐ brown/white 2   ☐ light blue/black 3   ☐ blue/white 3   ☐ orange/white 0

This is the same body style as #1374 with the flamethrower modification and Aurora was clearly using up extra bodies when they released this car. Different variations exist. The Cobra GT is the same as #1375 with the flamethrower modifications.

1496 (1196) Sand Van Dune Buggy "Flamethrower" 1971-72
(BODY/TOP)

☐ lime/green 3   ☐ pink/purple 3

The Sand Van Dune Buggy is California styled with cathedral rear windows and a two tone top. It has the modifications for the flamethrower option added. Superfat sponge tires were stock items. The body is that of the Dune Buggy #1398/#1399.

<u>Tuff Ones Two for One Specials</u>

<u>Assorted Carded Thunderjets</u>

54

Assorted Carded Thunderjets

Carded Thunderjet bodies (above and below)

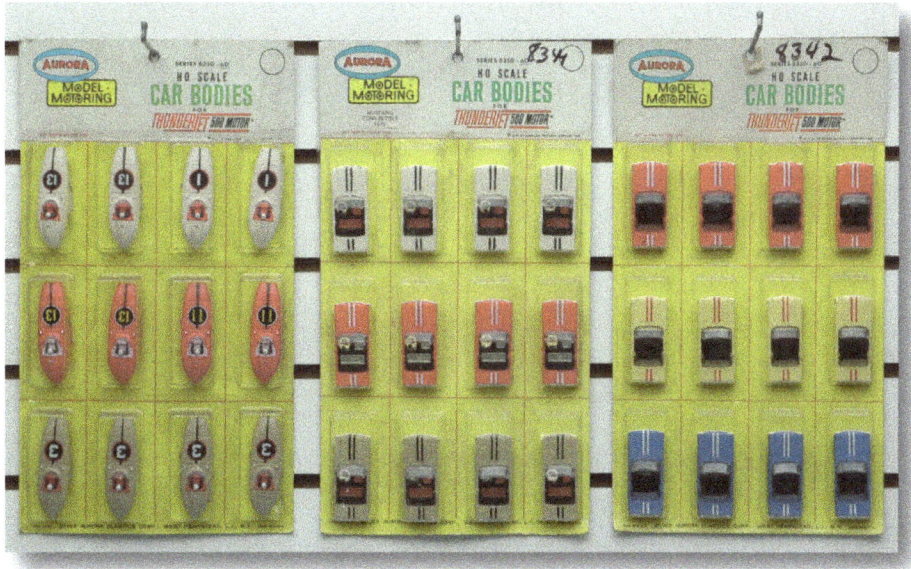

Chapter 5
Ford/Aurora

Aurora was always looking for new marketing strategies. They teamed up with the Ford Motor Company. In the first Ford-Aurora Grand National, thousands of dealers all over America participated. "The top tie-in of all time" would be a fair way of describing the Ford-Aurora In-Store Racing Promotion of 1962. Over a million contestants competed in thousands of stores from coast to coast. Millions more stood around and awatched, and rooted, and bought Model Motoring sets, cars, and accessories. All through the spring and summer—during the worst selling months of the year—stores displayed their "Headquarters" banners, hung their "Grand National" pennants over their "Official Circuit" layouts, ran hundreds of "Racing Tonite" ads in their local papers. Never before has a hobby product enjoyed such unforgettable brand identification at the point of sale. Never before has a hobby product so pre-conditioned its market for the Christmas pay-off. Publicized by a magnificent story in the July 3rd issue of *Look* magazine, the Ford-Aurora Grand National is reaching its climax at this very moment, August 1962.

1962 Ford/Aurora Grand Nationals

Aurora foot the bill for the entire In-Store Racing program. Only full time hobby dealers were allowed to participate and they were sent an entire packet of in-store racing promotional materials. The hobby stores had representation from the local Ford dealerships as well as using community leaders as judges and turn marshals. The kids had to race Aurora Ford products exclusively and rules were pretty strict with regard to modification of the cars and qualifying race times. Each hobby store had a winner who competed against other hobby store winners in their state, to establish a single state winner. Those winners then competed to establish (8) regional winners. The regional winners competed in NY the day before the national race. The (4) best racers then raced on national television for the Grand Prize—a brand new Ford automobile. All along the way special prizes and promotional material were offered. This program was an immediate success and ran for several years.

The 1962 Grand Nationals were held live on *The Today Show,* hosted by Jack Lescoulie, on NBC, August 21st.

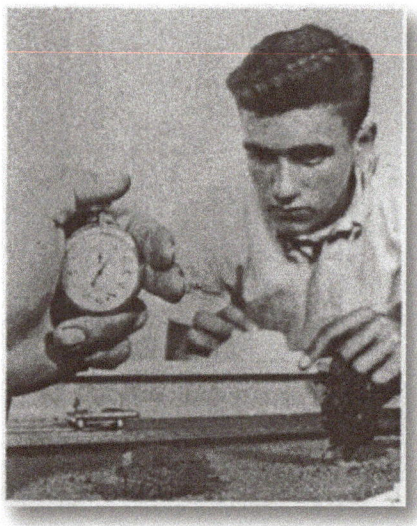

Winner:	Henry Harnish, New Jersey
Grand Prize:	1962 Ford Thunderbird convertible
	Championship Trophy
Regional Prize:	Engraved Wrist Watch
	Supply of Aurora Model Motoring products
	Special racing shirt
State Prize:	State Championship Trophy
	Special racing shirt
Store Prize:	"Top Driver 1962" Championship Trophy
Store Promo:	Ford "406" decal and number
	Model Motoring membership card
Rules:	Official Circuit, only Ford Aurora stock cars.

In-Store Racing Program materials containing trophies, banners, decal sheets, streamers, membership cards, official entries, rules, and scorecard materials.

1962 winner—Henry Harnish

1962 Regional award

1962 In Store Promotional Package

1962 Second Prize winner awards
Phil Schultz of Illinois

1962 Ford/Aurora License

1962 contestants with decals

In 1963, Aurora announced the Second Annual Ford/Aurora Grand National Model Motoring Competition, right on the heels of the highly successful program the previous year. Aurora used the proven advertizing in newspapers and magazines from the 1962 program as a tie in to hobby dealers participating in the '63 program. There was a lot of press and Aurora marketed this strategy.

Aurora kept the rules the same in '63. Only full time hobby dealers were allowed to participate and they were sent an entire packet of in-store racing promotional materials. The hobby stores had representation from the local Ford dealerships as well as using community leaders as judges and turn marshals. The kids had to race Aurora Ford products exclusively and rules were pretty strict with regard to modification of the cars and qualifying race times. Each hobby store had a winner who competed against other hobby store winners in their state, to establish a single state winner. Those winners then competed to establish (8) regional winners. The regional winners competed the day before the national race and then the (4) best raced on national television for the Grand Prize—a brand new 1963 Ford Thunderbird Sports Roadster convertible. All along the way special prizes and promotional material were offered.

The 1963 Grand Nationals were held live on Johnny Carson's *The Tonight Show* on NBC, August 20th. Stirling Moss was Carson's guest and was interviewed prior to being Grand Marshal of the race.

Winner:	Ron Colerick, South Dakota
Grand Prize:	1963 Ford Thunderbird convertible
	Championship Trophy
Regional Prize:	Regional championship Trophy
	Supply of Aurora Model Motoring products
	Special racing shirt
State Prize:	State Championship Trophy
	Special racing shirt
Store Prize:	First Place checkered flag motif Championship Trophy
	2nd, 3rd, and 4th place trophies also given out
Store Promo:	Ford "427" decal and number
	Model Motoring competition license

Rules for the races. Official Circuit for state and regional time trials. Only Ford Aurora stock cars. In-Store Racing Program materials containing trophies, banners, decal sheets, streamers, competition driver's licenses, official entries, rules, and scorecard materials. The A-1 Ford Used Car Lot cardboard counter display was offered free to all stores participating.

1963 First Prize winner—Ron Colerick's awards

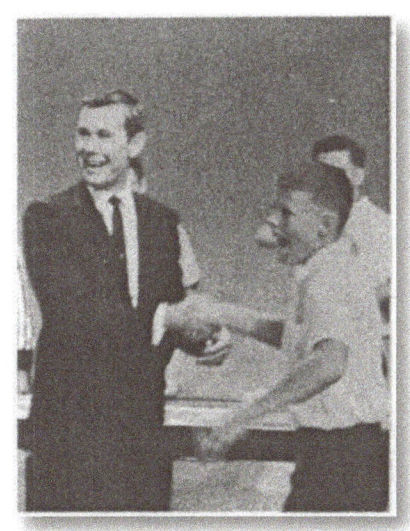

Ronnie winning on
The Tonight Show

***1963 Second Prize winner—
Phil Schultz's (again) awards***

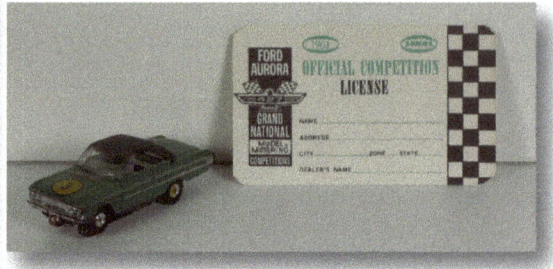

***1963 Second Prize-winner—
Phil Schultz's winning Ford***

***1963 Second Prize winner—
Phil Schultz' shirt and winning Ford***

The third Ford/Aurora Grand Nationals. At the New York Toy Fair, an Aurora Show Newspaper headline read "Ford and Aurora Introduce Exciting New Racing Format. "BEAT THE CHAMP" Competition Looms As Best In-Store Racing Program Ever Held!" Aurora hired Glenn "Fireball" Roberts as their spokesman for the contest and established a time the contestants had to beat. The car used was a new model being introduced that April by Ford.

Simultaneously Ford and Aurora both introduced their brand new Ford Mustang on the same day. You had to buy the Mustang HO car to enter the race. The in-store portion of the contest lasted only 2 weeks. Everyone who beat the champ received a certificate and a lapel pin in the shape of a stopwatch with a Mustang on it. Fireball Roberts died in a car crash that spring and it tarnished the Ford/Aurora competition. All of the paperwork was changed to just "Beat the Champ" and Glenn Roberts name was removed from the promotional material.

Each hobby store had a winner and the 48 fastest times sent to Aurora were picked to establish a single state winner. Those winners then competed, not in person, but on official layouts, to establish (8) regional winners. The regional winners raced together in NY and the top (4) raced on national television for the Grand Prize—a brand new 1964 ½ Ford Mustang Hardtop. All along the way special prizes and promotional material were offered.

The 1964 Grand Nationals were held live on Steve Allen's *I've Got a Secret* show on CBS. Stirling Moss was again the Grand Marshal of the race.

Winner:	Tom Kilduff, Pennsylvania
Grand Prize:	1964 ½ Ford Mustang Hardtop Championship Trophy
Regional Prize:	Engraved Ford/Aurora stopwatch Ford Aurora tee Shirt
State Prize:	State Championship Trophy
Store Prize:	First Place Gold Lapel pin "I Beat the Champ" card
Store Promo:	silver plated lapel pin Model Motoring competition license
Rules:	Official Circuit for state and regional time trials. Only Ford Aurora Mustang hardtops and convertibles.

In-Store Racing Program materials containing lapel pins, banners, flyers, I Beat the Champ cards, official entries, rules, and scorecard materials.

1964 Winner Tom Kilduff

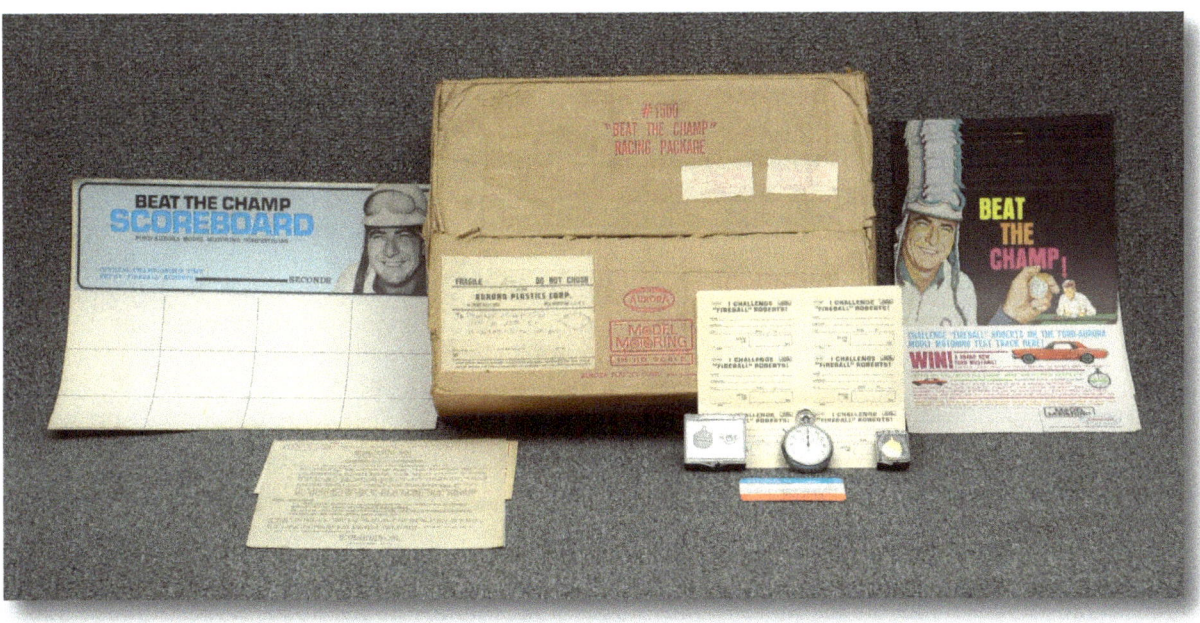

1964 In-Store Promotional Package

1964 In-Store Racing Banner

1964 Store Awards

1964 Regional Award (engraved)
Winner Mike Ferrell

The fourth Ford/Aurora Grand Nationals. Aurora had a track record of running a successful program for 3 years and they played that up big. As an added incentive for kids to enter, Car Craft Magazine was offering the winner a free trip to the 6th Annual NHRA Winter Nationals Championship Drag Races in Pomona California. This marked the first time Aurora gave the dealers an incentive. $500.00 of free merchandise to the dealer who runs the best in-store program. You had to buy the Mustang HO car to enter the race.

The entire program was run in 8 weeks. The in-store, state, and regional races were run as best time trials. As in the past, the best (8) regional winners raced on national television for the Grand Prize—a brand new 1966 Ford Mustang 2+2 fastback. All along the way special prizes and promotional material were offered. When the dealers signed up they received a special promotions package and a minimum order of Competition Pacs. These pacs are highly sought after today and they contain (2) candy plated Mustang fastback bodies, along with a controller, bottle of tire trac, and decals. The pacs were sold only to the hobby shops who ran the Ford Aurora races.

The 1965 Grand Nationals were held live on *The Mike Douglas Show* in Philadelphia. The boys raced competitively with HO and 1/32 scale cars at Aurora's retail Raceway on Hempstead Turnpike in West Hempstead, stayed in a fancy hotel in NY City, and were chauffeured to Philadelphia for the televised finals. Stirling Moss was again the Grand Marshal of the race.

Winner:	John Seeley, South Dakota
Grand Prize:	1966 Ford Mustang 2+2 Fastback
	Championship Trophy
Regional Prize:	All expense paid trip for (2) to NY City
State Prize:	Championship trophy
Store Prize:	Store Championship Trophy
Store Promo:	Gold Medal (one for each of the (8) week contest)
Rules:	Official Circuit for store, state, and regional time trials. Only Ford Aurora Mustangs.

In-Store Racing Program materials were at a wholesale cost of $80.00 to the dealer. The package contained (24) Competition Pacs, the official layout track sections, (1) store trophy, and (8) gold medals. The package also contained assorted banners, flyers, streamers, official entries, rules, and scorecard materials.

1965 winner, John Seeley

1965 Store Award Competition Pac and other prizes

The fifth Ford/Aurora Grand Nationals proved to be the last. I'm not sure why, but perhaps it had a lot to do with the fact that discount toy stores were springing up all over, This destroyed the loyalty between the hobby shops and slot car buyers, as everyone wanted to pay the cheapest price.

For 1966, Aurora wanted to cut down on the length of time the hobby stores had to run the in-store programs. They suggested a (4) week program instead of the usual (8). You had to run a 1967 Aurora Ford '67 Thunderbird. This car was brand new by Aurora and was only offered to those shops who ran the program.

The entire program was run in 4 weeks. The in-store races were run on any track the store wanted to run on. Aurora asked for the road course drawing and the time it took the winner to complete 25 laps. They then used a formula to determine the winners from each state. Then regional time trials were run to determine the (8) regional winners. As in the past, the best (4) of the eight regional winners raced on national television for the Grand Prize—a brand new 1967 Ford Mustang GT 2+2. All along the way special prizes and promotional material were offered. When the dealers signed up they received a special promotions package. The winner of each store competition received a special edition chrome plated 1967 Aurora Thunderbird.

The 1966 Grand Nationals were held live on the NY syndicated kids show, Sonny Fox' *Wonderama,* on WNEW. The boys raced with HO and 1/32 scale cars at Aurora's Raceway on Hempstead Turnpike in W. Hempstead and stayed in a fancy hotel in NY City. Stirling Moss was the Grand Marshal of the race.

Winner:	Rick Hanna, Indiana
Grand Prize:	1967 Ford Mustang GT 2+2
	Championship Trophy
Regional Prize:	All expense paid trip for (2) to NY City
	Watch inscribed with the Ford Aurora logo.
	Ford-Aurora tee Shirt
State Prize:	Championship trophy
Store Prize:	chrome plated 1967 Aurora Thunderbird
Rules:	any Circuit for store, state and regional time trials. Only Ford Aurora '67 T'birds sold exclusively at participating dealers.

In-Store Racing Program package (1) store metallized '67 T'bird. Two dozen brand new Ford '67 Thunderbirds for the races. The package also contained assorted banners, flyers, streamers, official entries, rules, and scorecard materials.

1966 Store Award '67 Thunderbird and Rick Hanna's winning Ford Mustang 2+2

**Chapter 6
O Gauge**

The The Aurora "O" gauge cars were an attempt to have an accessory that would compliment the popular model railroads of the day. To my knowledge, there has never been a railroad crossing section to mate up with 027 trains. Many of these cars were sold and used as static displays on railroad layouts. They used the thunderjet pancake motor in a larger chassis arrangement. The motor was under powered for the size of the car. They did not run well and only lasted in the catalogs for (2) years. The body styles were designed around a hot rod theme. They are a very popular item among collectors today. Sets, cars, track and accessories complemented the line. To get rid of excess track, Aurora made a transition piece in 1967 to go from O to HO. This piece was included in some sets or sold separately.

1751 Pickup   1752 Chopped Sedan   1753 '36 Ford   1754 '57 Chevy

1755 '39 Merc.   1756 '57 T'Bird   1757 '27 'T' Rod   1758 '32 Deuce Coupe

Aston Martin DB-4   Mustang Fastback

**A. C. Gilbert James Bond set cars. These were bodies made by Gilbert
and their chassis was a flop so they bought O gauge chassis
from Aurora to save the set. Early Gilbert cars have a white Gilbert chassis.**

(See rarity information on page 73.)

1751 (1851 boxed) '31 Ford Hot Rod Pickup 1963-69

The Hot Rod Pickup is a one piece molded body with a separate chrome grill and engine. Front bumper tips are known to be broken. The top is black and there is a driver inside. There is a set of decals provided with the car.

☐ **yellow/red 3**   ☐ **turquoise/black 3**   ☐ **red/tan 3**   ☐ **white/red 3**   ☐ **tan/red 3**

1752 (1852 boxed) Ford "Hot Pepper" Chopped Sedan 1963-69

This is a one piece molded body with "glass" all around. The front and rear bumpers are separate chrome pieces and are often missing as they are very fragile. The motor is also a separate chrome piece. This car is reminiscent of the gangster cars of the '30's. There is a set of decals provided with the car.

☐ *yellow 3*   ☐ *turquoise 3*   ☐ *red 3*   ☐ *white 3*   ☐ *tan 3*   ☐ *gray 2*

1753 (1853 boxed) '36 Ford Convertible Coupe 1963-69

The '36 Ford is a molded one piece body with fragile front and rear chrome bumpers. There is a spare tire mount on the trunk lid. There also is a driver inside the car. The top is always black. The drivers can vary in color and do not affect the value. There is a set of decals provided with the car.

☐ **yellow/red 3**   ☐ **turquoise/red 3**   ☐ **red/tan 3**   ☐ **white/red 3**   ☐ **tan/red 3**

1754 (1854 boxed) '57 Chevy Coupe 1963-69

Aurora's first attempt at the popular '57 Chevy. Why they never made a tjet version of this car I'll never know. It would have been a big seller. The Chevy is a one piece molded body with separate chrome bumpers front and rear. A glass piece is inside and the car has no interior. There is a set of decals provided with the car.

☐ **yellow 2**   ☐ **turquoise 1**   ☐ **red 2**   ☐ **white 2**   ☐ **tan 2**   ☐ **gray 1**

1755 (1855 boxed) '49 "Merc" Rod 1964-69

The '49 Mercury is a one piece molded body with separate front and rear chrome plated bumpers. The engine is exposed and there is full "glass" inside. There is a set of decals provided with the car.

☐ *yellow 3* ☐ *turquoise 3* ☐ *red 3* ☐ *white 3* ☐ *tan 3*

1756 (1856 boxed) '57 "Bird" Rod 1964-69

The Thunderbird is a one piece molded body with separate front and rear chrome plated bumpers. The top is black and there is a driver inside. There is no hood over the exposed engine. The rear wheel wells give the appearance of being cut but most of the time this is original. There is a set of decals provided with the car.

☐ *yellow/red 2*   ☐ *turquoise/gray 2*   ☐ *red/tan 2*   ☐ *white/light blue/dark blue 2*   ☐ *tan/red 2*

1757 (1857 boxed) 27 "T" Rod 1964-69

The "T" Rod is a one piece molded body with a lot of chrome detail added to it. There is a chrome plated engine and radiator up front. Quite often, the Indian head radiator ornament is broken off. There is a small chrome plated rear bumper as well as a roll bar behind the driver. There are different interior color combinations. The color of the driver can vary and does not affect the value of the car. There is a set of decals provided with the car.

- ☐ *yellow/tan 3*
- ☐ *yellow/green 3*
- ☐ *red/tan 3*
- ☐ *white/green 3*
- ☐ *tan/red 3*
- ☐ *tan/green 3*
- ☐ *tan/brown 3*
- ☐ *turquoise/black 3*

1758 (1858 boxed) '32 "Deuce" Rod 1965-69

The '32 Deuce is a one piece molded body with an exposed chrome plated engine. The radiator is often broken as is the small fragile rear chrome plated bumper. There is a set of decals provided with the car.

☐ yellow 3   ☐ turquoise 3   ☐ red 3   ☐ white 3   ☐ tan 3

The following two cars were actually made by the A. C. Gibert Company for their 1/32 modular James Bond Slot Car Set. They had production problems with a chassis they were developing and they had to scramble to meet orders. They went to Aurora and bought up some of the O gauge chassis inventory and modified their bodies to fit. A nice complement to the O gauge line, they are clearly a cheaper plastic and quality to Aurora. The Gilbert chassis is harder to find than the Aurora one. *(Photographs on page 65.)*

JAMES BOND ASTON MARTIN DB5 1965

The Aston Martin is a one piece molded body with a clear windshield. There is a chrome plated bumper front and rear, as well as a plated shield on back.

☐ red 4   ☐ blue 4

'67 MUSTANG 2+2 1965

The Mustang is a one piece molded body with a clear windshield. There is a chrome plated bumper in the front and back.

☐ red 4   ☐ blue 4

Chapter 7
Cigarbox

In 1968 Aurora announced their new series of HO scale cars called Cigarbox. Originally packaged in a flip front simulated cigar box, one could hardly resist the comparison to the wildly successful Matchbox™ cars of the day. Aurora, for the most part, took existing tooling for the slot cars and modified it to have shorter screw posts to accommodate the Cigarbox diecast chassis. The bodies remained plastic with additional slight modifications front and rear for the metal bumpers cast into the rolling diecast chassis. The cars were initially under a dollar when thunderjets were $2.98 list. HO slot car racers bought these cars, discarded the chassis, and adapted them to the tjet chassis for racing to save money. Shim the screw posts and you were ready to go. The first Cigarbox cars had the chassis screwed on and later they were pressed in rivets that could easily be removed. All Cigarbox cars have standard tjet tires and metal rims, with the exception of the Formula I cars, that have larger treaded tires and metal rims.

6101 Stingray 1968

SETS

6431 -1-	Cigarbox City #1 Set	(2) cars, track, stackable boxes	1969
6432 -1-	Cigarbox City #2 Set	(2) cars, more track, more stackable boxes	1969
6433 -1-	Cigarbox City #3 Set	(2) cars, most track, most stackable boxes	1969

GIFT SETS

6411 -1-	The All Americans	12 US cars	1968
6412 -1-	The International Champions	12 Foreign cars	1968
6413 -1-	The Dazzling Dozen	12 metallic plated cars	1968

6104 Ford J Car 1968

6105 Ford GT 1968

CARS

Rarity guide for all colors is shown below.

-3- yellow	-3- red	-3- white	-3- tan	
-3- turquoise	-2- blue	-2- green	-1- grey	
-1- black	-1- watermelon	-3- plated peach	-3- plated plum	-3- plated gold

6101	Stingray	1968	6102	Ferrari Berlinetta	1968
6103	Mako Shark	1968	6104	Ford J Car	1968
6105	Ford GT	1968	6106	Lola GT	1968
6107	Ford XL500	1968	6108	Toronado	1968
6109	Riviera	1968	6110	'67 Thunderbird	1968
6111	Dino Ferrari	1968	6112	Porsche 904	1968
6113	Cobra GT	1968	6114	Chaparral	1968
6115	Camaro	1969	6116	Cougar	1969
6117	McLaren Elva	1969	6118	Mustang Convertible	1969
6120	Mangusta	1968			

The following six Formula 1 cars were too narrow to be adapted to the tjet chassis. They were an entirely new body design.

6121	Formula I Lola Ford	1968	6122	Formula I Ferrari	1968
6123	F. I Cooper Maserati	1968	6124	Formula I Lotus Ford	1968
6125	Formula I Honda	1968	6126	Formula I BRM	1968

Standard Cigarbox issues *continued....*

6127	XKE Jaguar	1969	6128	Mustang Hardtop	1969
6129	AC Cobra	1969	6130	Firebird	1969
6131	Willys Gasser	1969	6132	Hot Rod	1969
6133	Cheetah	1969	6153	Volkswagen Bug	1969
0053	Ice Cream Truck	1972			

6106   Lola GT   1968

6109 Riviera and 6110 '67 Thunderbird

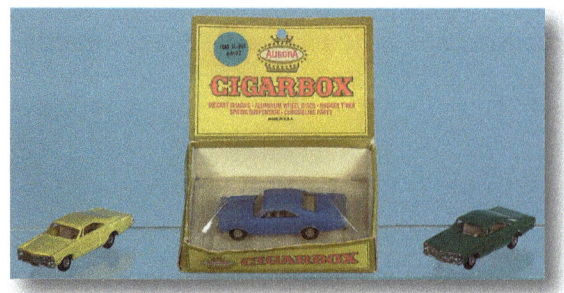
6107 Ford XL500   1968

6110 '67 T'Bird

6116 Cougar, 6113 Cobra Gt, 6117 McLaren Elva

6111 Dino Ferrari and 6112 Porsche 904

6118 Mustang and Dune Buggys

6111 Dino Ferrari's

The following vehicles were never made. (#6134-#6150)
Prototypes of some do exist in different places.

6134 Dump Truck	6135 Cement Mixer
6136 Tow Truck	6137 Jeep
6138 Bus	6139 Bulldozer
6140 Front End Loader	6141 Road Grader
6142 GMC Stake Truck	6143 Panel Truck
6144 GMC tractor	6145 Van Trailer
6146 Tank Trailer	6147 Flat Bed Trailer
6148 Oil Truck	6149 Moving Van
6150 Ford Stake Truck	

Assorted Cigarbox cars
(TOP ROW: **standard**; CENTER ROW: **Formula 1s**;
BOTTOM ROW: **Jaguar and 53 Ice Cream Truck**)

Bookshelf Case (vinyl) and trays

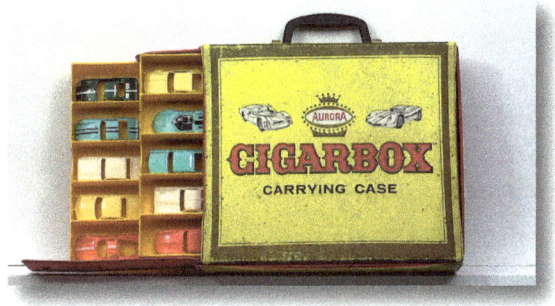

Deluxe Case (2) trays

ACCESSORIES

6421	-3-	Bookshelf Case (vinyl)	1969
6422	-2-	Deluxe Case (2) trays)	1969
6430	-4-	Speed Track (6 foot)	1969

Chapter 8
Speedline-Speedsters

In 1968 Aurora announced still another new series of HO scale cars called Speedline. Originally packaged on a see through blister card, or bubble pack. They were clearly introduced to compete with the successful free wheeling toys of the '60's such as Mattel's Hot Wheels™ and Topper's Johnny Lightning™ cars. Aurora, for the most part, took existing tooling for the slot cars and modified it to have shorter screw posts to accommodate the Cigarbox diecast chassis to which they then added larger hard plastic wheels. The bodies remained plastic and most were candy plated along with additional slight modifications front and rear for the metal bumpers cast into the rolling diecast chassis. The molds were also modified to accommodate the larger wheels. This explains why some tjet cars have larger molded wheel wells than others of the same body style (ex: #1388 Camaro and #1380 Mako Shark). The cars were list priced under a dollar when thunderjets were $2.98 list. HO slot car racers bought these cars, discarded the chassis, and adapted them to the tjet chassis for racing to save money. Shim the shorter screw posts and you were ready to go. Most Speedline cars had the chassis had pressed in rivets that could easily be removed. All Speedline cars have the same oversize wheels. The plated versions all had a wide stripe down the center. The Aurora Speedsters came out as a way to get rid of excess stock in bodies and chassis. They were a cost reduced version that was not plated, painted or detailed and was left in the odd but interesting base colors for plating. Peach, pumpkin, salmon colors all are from this series. An additional variation of the speedline had a hole molded into the roof. This allowed air to rush through as the car sped down the track and a whistling sound could be heard. I don't think it was successful.

SETS

6905 -5-	2 In 1 Crisscross Race Set	(2) cars, flex track, slingshot starters.	1968-69
6910 -5-	2 In 1 Stunt and Drag Set	(2) cars, flex track, supports.	1968-69
6915 -3-	2 In 1 Loop and Bank Set	(2) cars, flex track, returns, supports.	1968-69

GIFT SETS

-1-   (6) car Pack

Rarity guide for all the different colors of Speedline/Speedsters.

-1- purple	-3- white	-2- mustard	-3- yellow (shades)
-2- lemon	-2- blue (shades)	-1- black	-1- lime
-1- pumpkin	-2- green (shades)	-2- orange	-1- salmon
-2- peach	-1- gray	-4- plated red	-3- plated blue
-2- plated green	-4- plated peach	-3- plated plum	-4- plated gold

CARS

6801 Stingray	6802 Ferrari Berlinetta	6803 Mako Shark
6804 Ford J Car	6805 Ford GT	6806 Lola GT
6807 Ford XL500	6108 Toronado	6109 Riviera
6810 '67 Thunderbird	6811 Dino Ferrari	6812 Porsche 904
6813 Cobra GT	6114 Chaparral	6815 Camaro
6816 Cougar	6117 McLaren Elva	6818 Mustang Convertible
6819 Dune Buggy	6820 Mangusta	

The following six Formula I cars were too narrow to be adapted to the tjet chassis. They were an entirely new body design.

6821 Formula I Lola Ford	6822 Formula I Ferrari	6823 Form. I Cooper Maserati
6824 Formula I Lotus Ford	6825 Formula I Honda	6826 Formula I BRM

Standard issue cars continued........

6827 XKE Jaguar	6828 Mustang Hardtop	6829 AC Cobra
6830 Firebird	6831 Willys Gasser	6132 Hot Rod
6835 Cheetah	6853 Volkswagen Bug	6854 Charger
6855 Torino	6856 Alfa Romeo	

Assorted Speedline and Speedster cars. Note wheel sizes and openings.

The following were cataloged but never made. Prototypes do exist for some of the cars listed. All are shown to be announced in the 1969 Toy Fair catalog

6857 Batmobile	6858 Black Beauty	6861 GMC Van
6862 Dump Truck	6863 Stake Body Truck	6864 Tow Truck
6865 Cement Mixer		

SUPER SPEEDLINE

All below cataloged but never made (1969)

6781 Super '31 Ford Hot Rod Pickup	6782 Super '32 Ford Chopped Sedan
6783 Super '36 Ford Convertible	6784 Super '57 Chevy Stocker
6785 Super '49 Mercury Rod	6786 Super '57 T'Bird Rod
6787 Super '27 'T' Rod	6788 Super '31 Deuce Rod

ACCESSORIES

	-5-	Slingshot Starters	1968
	-5-	The Finish Line	1968
	-5-	The Criss-Cross	1968
	-5-	Speedline flexible (2) Lane Track	1968
	-5-	The Hop Up Kit	1968
	-5-	The Barrel Jump	1968
6877	-5-	90 deg 2 Lane Banked Curve	1969
6878	-5-	Starting Pylon	1969
6879	-5-	Speed Track Slick	1969
6895	-2-	Carrying Case (vinyl cover) holds 15 cars	1968
6925	-4-	Rattle Trap and Base	1969
6926	-4-	Flash Back Pit Stop	1969
6931	-5-	Flash Back Lap Counter	1969

Assorted Speedline and Speedster cars. Plated and molded.

Assorted Speedline and Speedster cars. Note the top row of Formula I cars and the different shades of standard colors.

Assorted carded Speedline cars molded, plated, and Hop up kits.

SPEEDSTERS 1971-77

Any colors and combinations can be packaged as Aurora did not catalog this product. They were using up old stock of tjet bodies and speedline chassis. These are very cheap and often do not contain the windshields and chrome plated pieces. There are some rare colors that were packaged this way and they do command higher prices even though the screw posts are shorter and they are unpainted. Some of the tougher colors are grey and black along with many shades of standard colors.

Super Speedsters (3) packs. Cheaply manufactured in desirable colors

Razzy Racers in their original packaging.

RAZZY RACERS 1971

In 1971 Aurora found themselves looking to decrease inventory where they could. A product that the Research and Development team came up with was the Razzy Racers. These toys enabled Aurora to use up excess Cigarbox chassis they had laying around. These cars had injection molded bodies that were wildly painted and mounted over a cigarbox stock chassis with a pipe shaped plastic tube riveted to it. They rolled and were powered by a balloon that was inflated and put over the top opening. A razzer, much like the kind you would use as a New Year's Eve noisemaker, was at the back end and made noise as the balloon deflated and the car traveled across the floor. Cool idea, they made (6) different cars and a few accessories. I'm not sure of the success of the product, but they are hard to come by today probably due to low volume production.

5529	-3-	Sprint Special Set—Starting Gate, 2 Racers, 2 inflator valves, 4 balloons
5530	-3-	Jet Rally Set—Air pump, starting gate, 2 racers, 2 valves, 4 balloons
5531	-3-	Air pump with inflator valve
5532	-2-	Razzy Racers w/ 2 balloons
5533	-2-	Razzy Racers w/ inflator valve and 2 balloons
5534	-3-	Starting Gate

> **Chapter 9
> Other Scales**

AURORA 1/32 BIG CAR RACING

Aurora ventured into the very lucrative field of 1/32 scale slot cars in 1965. The company bought K&B, who was a decent manufacturer of these other scales. We will only list those cars and sets that were listed under the Aurora name. Many of the parts were, in fact, made by other companies for Aurora. For the most part, the Aurora cars were a flop and not competitive at the track. That does not hinder the fact that they are highly sought after collectibles today. Aurora called them A-Jets. The A stood for Americans and the cars carried an American Flag on the doors. In 1966 Aurora tooled up and released their own 1/32 sets on the market. In 1970 Aurora re-released the 1/32 sets for a second try at a limited market.

SETS

3200	-3-	American Classic figure 8	1966-68
3201	-3-	World Championship Dual 8	1966-67
3202	-2-	Continental Giant 2 lane home raceway	1966
3203	-2-	International 1000 giant 4 lane home raceway	1966
3204	-1-	Thundercycle Race Set w/blue track	1967
3301	-3-	Stinger Race Set figure 8	1970-71
3302	-3-	Big Bank Race Set, 2 cars w/(2) extra bodies	1970
3303	-3-	The Snake Race Set w/(2) 180 degree Banked turns	1970-71
3304	-1-	Wheelie Trike Race Set w/2 Wheelie Trikes	1971
3305	-3-	Riverside Race Set, 2 cars w/(2) extra bodies	1971

3253 -3- Mustang 2+2 Fastback

3252 -3- Pontiac GTO

3251 -3- Ford GT

Thundercycles

3252 -3- Pontiac GTO

Wheelie Trike

Ferrari 612 and McLaren M12

Mustang 2+2 and Comet Eliminator

CARS

#		Name	Colors	Years
3251	-3-	Ford GT	white/blue red yellow	1966-67
3252	-3-	Pontiac GTO	white blue red yellow	1965-67
3253	-3-	Mustang 2+2 Fastback	white blue red yellow	1966-67
3254	-1-	Corvair Corsa	yellow	1965-67
3255	-2-	Plymouth Barracuda	white blue red yellow	1965-67
3256	-1-	Chaparral	white	1966-67
3257	-2-	Cobra GT Coupe	white blue red yellow	1966-67
3258	-1-	Comet Eliminator	red	1966-67
3266	-2-	Thundercycle	red yellow	1967-69
3350		1/32 car assortment		1971
3351	-4-	Ferrari 612	blue red orange	1970-71
3352	-4-	McLaren M12	blue red orange	1970-71
3353	-3-	Mirage Coupe		1970-71
3354	-3-	Ferrari 312 Coupe		1970-71
3355	-3-	Porsche 917		1970

Continued on next page.

Aurora 1/32 Big Car Racing (continued)

Cars (continued)

3356	-3-	TI 22	1970
3357	-0-	Mirage Coupe w/lights (cataloged, never made)	1970
3357	-2-	Green Machine Wheelie Trike	1971
		green two tone metalflake	
3358	-0-	Ferrari 312 Coupe w/lights (cataloged, never made)	1970
3358	-2-	Chopper Chariot Wheelie Trike	1971
		purple/violet two tone metalflake	
3259	-3-	Lola T-70	1966-67
3260	-3-	Rover BRM	1966-67

The first cars were made and the following cars were planned.

3261	-0-	Buick Demolition Derby	1966-67
3262	-0-	Mercury Demolition Derby	1966-67
3263	-0-	Toronado	1966-67
3264	-0-	Mako Shark	1966-67

Track and Accessories

3210	-5-	plug in Speed Control w/Brake	1966-67
3211	-5-	10½ Straight Track	1967
3212	-5-	12" Straight Track	1966-67
3213	-5-	12" plug in Terminal Track	1966-67
3214	-5-	14" Radius 60 deg Curve Track	1966-67
3215	-5-	14" Radius 30 deg Curve Track	1966-67
3216	-5-	21" Radius 30 deg. Curve track	1966-67
3217	-5-	12" Squeeze Track	1966-67
3218	-5-	Criss Cross Track	1966-67
3219	-5-	12" Bump Track	1966-67
3220	-5-	Board Fence w/Billboard Signs	1966-67
3221	-5-	14" Radius 60 deg Spin Out Shoulders	1966-67
3222	-5-	21" Radius 30 deg. Spin Out Shoulders	1966-67
3223	-5-	Spin Out Shoulder Ends	1966-67
3224	-5-	Modular Bridge Posts (48 pcs)	1966-67
3225	-2-	Electric Lap Counter w/30 deg trip section	1966-67
3226	-5-	Country Bridge w/Track	1967
3227	-5-	Bridge Track without Sides	1967
3228	-5-	Modular Beam Set (32 Posts and 4 Beams)	1967
3229	-5-	Country Bridge Extensions	1967
3230	-5-	Guard Rail Set (8 pcs.)	1967
3249	-5-	18V DC Power Pack	1966
3310	-5-	Hand Controller 25 ohm	1970-71
3311	-5-	Hand Controller 7.5 ohm	1970
3312	-5-	12" Straight Track	1970-71
3313	-5-	12" plug in Terminal and Lap Counter Track	1970-71
3314	-5-	14" Radius 60 deg Curve Track	1970-71
3321	-5-	14" Radius 60 deg Spin Out Shoulders	1970-71
3323	-5-	Spin Out Shoulder Ends	1970-71
3330	-5-	Guard Rail Set (8 pcs.)	1970-71
3331	-5-	Banked Track Set 180 degrees	1970-71
3332	-5-	Trestle Set	1970-71
3349	-5-	Power Pack 6VDC	1970-71

POWERSLICKS

Powerslicks were advertised as controlled power and free wheeling action. They had a clutch motor that engaged and disengaged the motor giving longer battery and motor life. Yes, the set was powered by batteries. Four D Cell batteries thrust the cars over a multitude of sets. The tracks were plastic troughs and snapped together with connectors. The cars had chrome mag wheels and soft slicks. They were radical new designs and a sign of things to come with the AFX line.

SETS
2101	-3-	Hillclimber Set	1970-71
2102	-3-	Eliminator Drag Set	1970-71
2103	-3-	Twin Oval 60	1970
2104	-3-	Great Chase Set	1970
2106	-3-	Octopus Reverse and Race Set	1971
2107	-3-	Bumper Basher Race Set	1971

CARS
2151	-3-	Too Much	1970-71
2152	-3-	Turbo Turn On	1970-71
2153	-3-	Mod Rod	1970-71
2154	-3-	Drag'n Devil	1970-71
2155	-3-	Bad Bandito	1970-71
2156	-3-	Wild Winger	1970-71

Too Much's

Draggin' Devil's

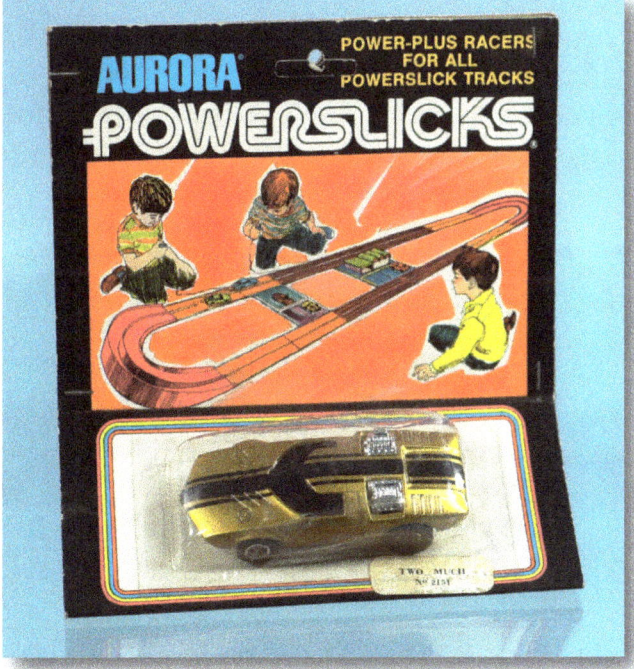

Packaging

Mod Rod—Wild Winger—Bad Bandito

Continued on next page.

Powerslicks (continued)

TRACK AND ACCESSORIES

2110	-3-	On Off Hand Power Switch	1970-71
2111	-3-	On Off Timer Hand Speed Control	1970
2112	-3-	On Off Christmas Tree Drag Starter	1970
2113	-3-	Power Station	1970-71
2114	-3-	Auxiliary Power People Station	1970
2116	-3-	Finish Flag Stand	1970
2117	-3-	Tunnel	1970
2118	-3-	Tunnel Horn Accessory	1970-71
2119	-3-	Hazzard Light Accessory	1970
2121	-4-	(4) 24" Straights	1970
2122	-4-	(8) 12" Straights	1970-71
2123	-3-	90 Deg. Single lane banked curve	1971
2124	-3-	180 Degree Single Lane Curve	1970-71
2125	-3-	(2) 180 Degree Dual Lane Curves	1970-71
2126	-3-	(2) Dual Lane Cross Overs	1970-71
2134	-3-	Power Lane Changer	1970
2135	-3-	Power Extender	1970
2136	-3-	24" Power Straight (2 power sections and adapters)	1971
2145	-3-	Track Package accessory	1970

THE IMPOSTERS

These cars are not really slot cars. They are so cool I had to add them to this book. They are an unassuming plastic 1/18 scale car on the outside. Wind up the purple gearshift key and get ready to rip. Release the rear tab under the bumper and they transform into an extended dragster and then accelerate across the floor. They look so much like large slot cars, they should have been.

5301	-2-	Volkswagon	yellow	1972
5302	-2-	Willys Coupe	pink	1972
5303	-2-	Pinto	blue	1972
5304	-0-	Gotcha Gremlin	blue (never made)	1972

Awesome transforming Volkswagon

Continued on next page.

THE IMPOSTERS *(continued)*

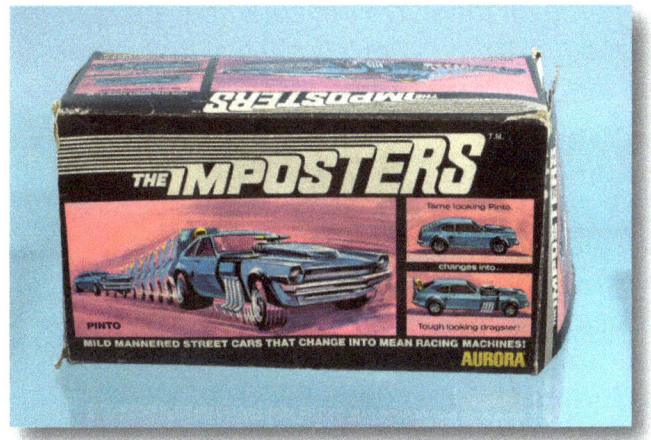

Typical Imposters packaging

Wild transforming Willy's Coupe

Powerful transforming Pinto

'N' Gauge Bus Sets

In 1968, Aurora ventured into the 'N' gauge area by having Minitrix (TM) make a line of busses and accessories with the Aurora name on them. I'm not sure how they started but the sets are quite nice and very popular among collectors today. There is a track that connects the 'N' gauge bus track to train tracks, thus integrating the whole system nicely into an 'N' gauge train empire.

4401	-2-	Postage Stamp City Bus Set	1968-69
4402	-2-	Postage Stamp City Bus Set with power pack	1968-69
4403	-1-	Postage Stamp Greyhound Bus set	1968-69
4403	-1-	Greyhound Bus w/silver trim, w/out silver trim, black or blue dog	1968-69
4404	-1-	Postage Stamp Greyhound Bus Set with power pack	1968-69
4411	-4-	Bus Straight Track Assortment	1968-69
4412	-4-	Bus Curved Track Assortment	1968-69
4413	-2-	Bus Bypass assortment	1968-69
4414	-3-	Bus 90 degree intersection Track Assortment	1968-69
4419	-2-	Bus Terminal Roadway Station	1968-69
4421	-2-	Bus Railroad Assortment	1968-69
4425	-2-	Bus Railroad Crossing Signal	1968-69
4426	-2-	Bus Relay for Railroad Crossing	1968-69
4431	-4-	Bus Speed Control	1968-69
4433	-2-	Bus System Traffic Light	1968-69
4435	-2-	Relay for Traffic Light	1968-69
4447	-2-	Relay for Bus Stop at Loading Zone	1968-69
4454	-4-	Bus Guard Rail Set	1968-69
4456	-4-	Bus Pier Set	1968-69
4481	-2-	City Bus yellow red green red/white	1968-69

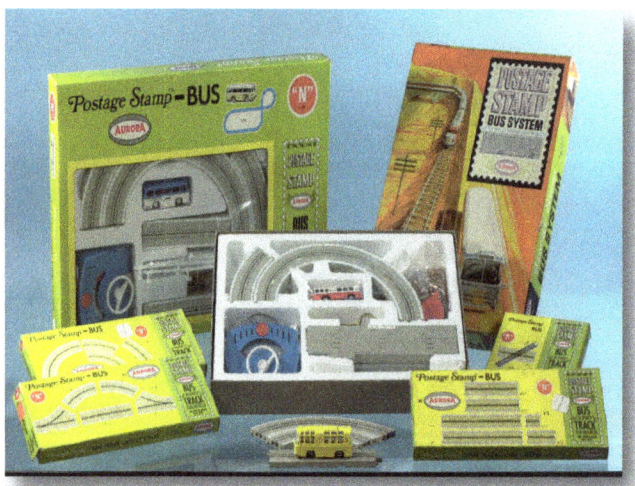

Bus sets and accessories

Greyhound variations and City Bus variations

**Chapter 10
Xlerators**

In 1973, Aurora introduced the Xlerators. These HO cars were new slotless racers. They advertised controlled racing for up to (4) cars. Each car contained a special diode that matched a diode in the terminal track. This enabled controlled racing anywhere on the track without guide pins or slots. Special push button controls let you speed up, slow down, or pass. The reality of it was that these cars did not work too well and were not a big seller. Some of them are very hard to find today and others are very common. The first Xlerators had a type I chassis which incorporated the much sought after, quadralam armature in it. Unfortunately a brass gear was swaged onto the armature shaft which hinders HO racers from modifying it easily. The type II chassis is basically an in line G-Plus type.

XL Ferrari GTO 1973

This is the first Xlerators car. It is essentially the Thunderjet Ferrari GTO #1368 with some slight mold modifications. It has small side wings in the front to help it slide around the turns of the Xlerators track.

2741 -0- red/white stripes #1   type I chassis

XL Ford GT 1973

This is basically the same as the thunderjet Ford GT #1374.

2742 -0- blue/black/white stripes #2   type I chassis

Ford J Car 1973

This is basically the same as the Thunderjet Ford J Car #1382.

2743 -5- orange/black/silver #3   type I chassis
      -5- yellow/black #3   type I or type II chassis
2783 -5- red/white/butterscotch   type II chassis
      -5- red/white/yellow #3   type II chassis

91

Chaparral 2F 1973

This is basically the same car as the Thunderjet Chaparral 2F #1410.

2744	-5-	white/lime #4	type I or type II chassis
2784	-5-	lime/black #4	type I or type II chassis
	-5-	butterscotch/black #4	type I or type II chassis
	-5-	bllblue/white #4	type I or type II chassis

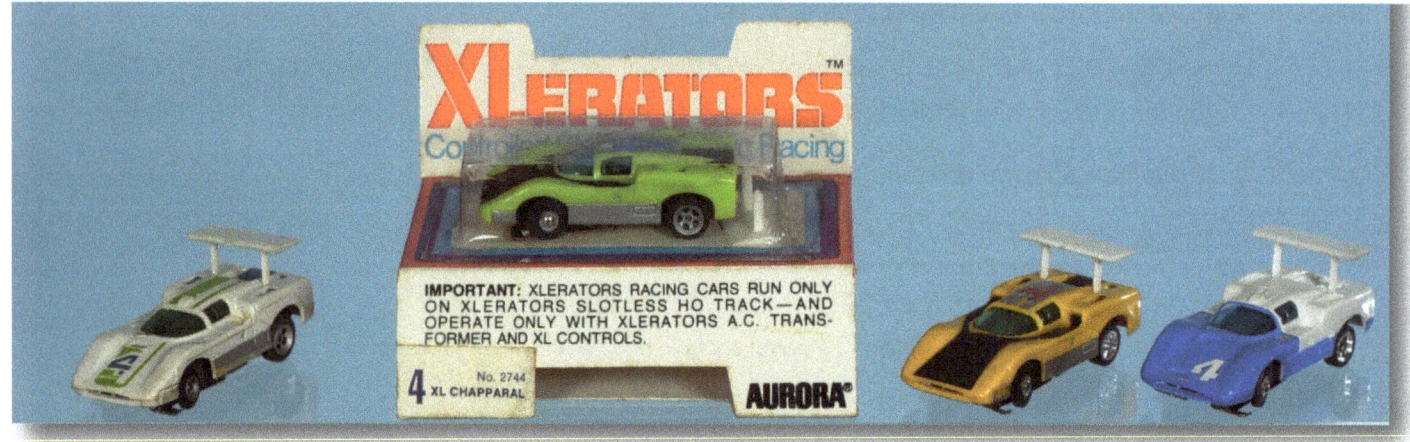

Camaro 1974

This is basically the same car as the thunderjet #1388.

2741	-3-	white/blue #1	type I chassis
	-3-	red/white #1	type I chassis
	-3-	orange/white #1	type I chassis

Firebird 1974

This is essentially the thunderjet #1402.

2742	-3-	yellow/black #2	type I chassis
	-3-	blue/bird #2	type II chassis
	-3-	blue/silver #2	type II chassis

Pro Stock Vega 1975

This is the first brand new body style made exclusively for the Xlerators. The car is a one piece molded body with a tinted windshield. It is a highly sought after car today.

2746   -2-   white/lime/black #3   type I chassis
        -2-   orange/red #3   type I chassis

Baja Blazer 1975

This is Aurora's second body style made exclusively for the Xlerators line. The pick up is a one piece molded body with a separate chrome plated front bumper. There is a chrome plated roll cage and (2) Bell helmeted drivers.

2747   -4-   white/black/red #4   type I or type II chassis
2785   -4-   white/red/blue #4   type I or type II chassis
        -4-   orange/blue/white #4   type I or type II chassis
        -4-   yellow/orange/black #4   type I or type II chassis

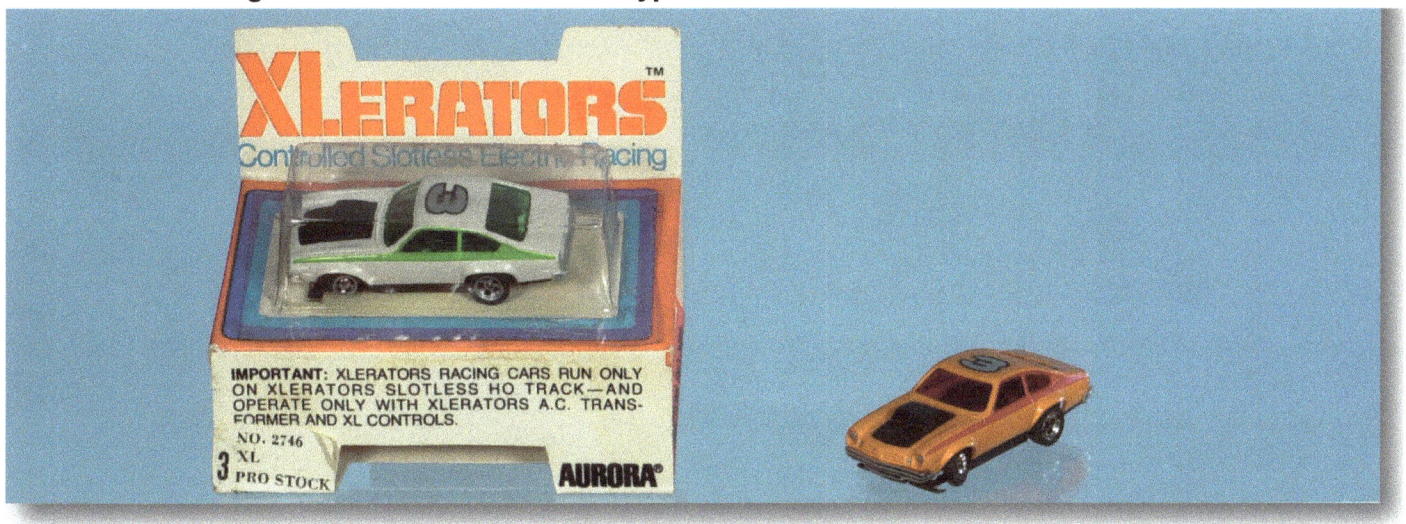

Cougar 1975

This is essentially the thunderjet Cougar #1389 with a new paint scheme.

2781 -3-   white/black/red #3   type I chassis
**   -3-   white/blue/red #3   type I chassis**
2786 -3-   butterscotch/blue/white #3   type II chassis

Willys Gasser 1975

This is essentially the thunderjet Willys #1401 with a new flamed paint scheme and the rear nerf bar missing.

2782 -2-   red/black/yellow flames #4   type I chassis
**   -2-   yellow/black/green flames #4   type II chassis**
**   -1-   white/black/blue flames #4   type II chassis**

Chapter 11 AFX

"The AFX cars are here" proclaimed the 1971 color catalog. First noted as A/FX. They stood for Aurora Factory Experimentals. These were cars so fast they left all the others at the starting line. The following cars will be cataloged in order of the type of car. It is very difficult to catagorize the AFX cars as the numerical order showed no rhyme or reason. The easiest way to use this guide is to verify the body style visually. Then check your car for the molded in number by removing the chassis. Then search for the molded in number. Check the colors made to find out what car you have. An example is the Chevy Nomad which came out in 1971. All chassis and color variations came out in the following years. All Nomads will be together starting with the molded in number (1760).

NON MAGNATRACTION

The first AFX cars were non-magnatraction and they featured the following:
- *dual wheelbase monococque chassis*
- *superfat sponge racing tires*
- *radially oriented magnets*
- *84% silver commutator brushs*
- *lightweight silver plated pickup shoes*
- *independently rotating front tires*
- *snap in top gear plate*
- *snap on painted body shells*
- *high performance gear ratio*
- *super detailed plated mag wheels*
- *self lubricating nylatron chassis*
- *steel front axle*
- *low road hugging center of gravity*

MAGNATRACTION

At the end of 1974 the magnatraction cars arrived. They had the extra added feature of the magnets being taller and close to the metal rails in the track. This allowed for magnetic traction and down force enabling the car to go faster without de-slotting. They featured the same as non-magnetraction plus:
- *taller magnets cut through the chassis*

G-PLUS

In 1976 G-Plus (gravity plus more) cars were offered. They had a new chassis design which included:
- *greatly increased traction*
- *30% reduction in lap time (faster)*
- *monocoque in line motor with brass bearings and bullet proof brushes*
- *reverse taper steel guide pin*
- *independent front wheels*
- *trued sponge slicks*

MAGNA-SONIC

These cars have a sound box that makes them sound like their motors are running. They are identical to the magnatraction with a few exceptions.
- *there is a sound box on the chassis in place of the gear clamp*
- *there is a dished out plastic idler gear*

ULTRA 5

These cars and sets were introduced in 1977 and had several new features. The name Ultra 5 comes from the 5 features outlined below:
- no slots
- precision steering
- variable speed control
- electro activated cars
- futuristic track

SUPER MAGNATRACTION

These were released in 1978 and changes in the chassis occured.
- Special high energy magnets
- low profile chassis (X frame)
- silver, gold, or metallic finish bodies

MAGNA STEERING

These cars worked with the Scre-e-echers sets introduced in 1976.
- They had a swivel front end that later was changed to fixed with a guide pin
- they were slotless
- G-Plus type chassis that was screwed into the bodies
- the sets were battery operated
- the product failed and fixed pins were added

SUPER G-PLUS

In 1978 Super G-Plus cars were offered. They had:
- high energy rare earth magnets
- high revving monocoque in line motor
- reverse taper steel guide pin
- independent front wheels
- trued sponge slicks

SPEED STEER SLOTLESS AND SLOTTED RACING

These cars and sets were introduced in 1979 and had several new features.
- no slots
- precision steering on the control
- front wheel steering action
- a slow moving car to act as a road blocker
- electro activated cars
- futuristic track

CATS EYES, BLAZIN' BRAKES, AND SPEED SHIFTER

These were all introduced in 1981 and had the following features:
- functional on/off headlights
- brakes and brake lights
- on/off operating overhead roof racks and forward/reverse action

AFX Cars

Ferrari Can Am 612 1971-74

The Ferrari is the first AFX car to be released. It is a one piece molded body with a chrome plated engine behind the Bell helmeted driver. This car came first with, and then without, the white wing. Some versions can come with and without nose and tail detailing. A variation is in side numbers or not.

1751	non-magnatraction	☐	-4-	red/white #15
		☐	-5-	yellow/red #15
		☐	-4-	yellow/purple #15
		☐	-4-	blue/white #15

Auto World McLaren XLR 1971-74

The Auto World McLaren is a one piece molded body with a white plastic wing on top. It can come with or without the wing or back detailing. The body has a painted race track running around it. The driver is Bell helmeted and the chrome plated engine is behind him. There can be varying number 54 sizes also.

1752	non-magnatraction	☐	-5-	orange/black #54
		☐	-5-	orange/grey #54
		☐	-3-	translucent yellow #54
		☐	-3-	yellow #54
		☐	-3-	blue/black green #54
		☐	-3-	blue #54
		☐	-1-	orange/blue #7

Porsche 917-10K Can Am 1974-79

This Porsche is a one piece molded body with a separate rear wing. The car has a square or rounded front air dam. There are stickers on the front, sides, and rear wing. The driver has a Bell helmet on. The interiors can be different colors.

1747	non-magnatraction	-4-	white/blue/red #16
1921	magnatraction	-4-	white/blue/red #16
	magnatraction	-1-	white/blue/red #23
3001	Ultra 5	-5-	white/blue/green/yellow #11

Lola T-260 Can-Am 1972-78

The T-260 is a one piece molded body with L&M sticker on the front and on the wing. The engine and roll bar are a separate chrome plated piece. The driver has a Bell helmet and the cockpit has a clear windshield.

1767	non-magnatraction	-5-	white/red/black L&M
1907	magnatraction	-5-	white/red/black L&M
3008	ultra 5	-4-	white/blue/green/yellow #39 (orange driver)
		-4-	white/blue/green/yellow #39 (white driver)

Porsche 510K "Can Am" 1973-78

The Porsche is a one piece molded body with a Bell helmeted driver and a chrome plated roll bar behind him. The front air dam is often broken and the removable rear spoiler is occasionally missing. There are paper stickers on the spoiler and on the sides. There can be detailing or no detailing on the front louvers. The louvers can be different sizes also.

1786	non-magnatraction	-5-	white/red/black #6
1915	magnatraction	-5-	white/red/black #6
		-5-	gold chrome/orange #4
		-4-	red/yellow/white #6 Sunoco
		-3-	orange/yellow #4 Sunoco

Continued on next page.

Porsche 510K "Can Am" 1973-78 *(continued)*

		☐ -3-	translucent yellow/blue #7 Sunoco
		☐ -3-	white/green/blue #5 Sunoco
3002	ultra 5	☐ -4-	white/blue/yellow/red #6
1743	G-Plus	☐ -3-	blue/yellow/red/black #6

Shadow Can-Am 1972-79

The Shadow is a very common car. The body is one piece molded with a separate wing on the back. The wing can come in varying heights. There is a sticker on the wing and a Bell helmeted driver.

1768	non-magnatraction	☐ -5-	black/white #101
1908	magnatraction	☐ -5-	black/white #101
		☐ -4-	white/yellow/orange #3
		☐ -5-	gold chrome/red #3
3007	ultra 5	☐ -2-	white/orange/black/yellow #3
1744	G-Plus	☐ -4-	white/yellow/orange/red #3
1784		☐ -4-	white/blue/red #3

Too Much 1971-74
Double Trouble 1976-83
Fly Mobile 1977-78

This car is a made up body by Aurora. It is a one piece molded body with a dark windshield and (2) chrome plated engines. There is also a chrome plated rear set of exhausts. There are different shades of this car in existence. The Double Trouble is a derivative of the Too Much car. It is a molded one piece body. The twin engines are chrome plated. The car is on a magna-steering chassis and was used in the battery operated Scre-e-echers Sets. The car was produced as a Scre-e-echer until 1977 and then re-issued in 1982 as a Lazer 2000 with the engines removed and the mold modified. The Fly Mobile is a derivative of the Too Much. It is a molded one piece body. The twin engines are chrome plated. The car is on a magna-steering fixed pin chassis and was used in the battery operated Scre-e-echers Sets.

#	Type	Rating	Colors
1754	non-magnatraction	-4-	orange/purple
		-4-	yellow/orange
		-3-	red/black
		-5-	green/metallic green
5788	magna-steering	-4-	yellow/orange/red #5
5808	magna-steering pin	-5-	yellow/orange/red (no number)
2010	Orion 2000	-4-	white/lime/green/yellow
2011	Saturn 2000	-4-	white/light purple/dark purple
5812	magna-steering pin	-4-	green/blue Fly Mobile

Turbo Turnon 1971-74
Terrible Turbo 1976-83
Spider Mobile 1977-78

This car is a made up body by Aurora. It is a one piece molded body with a dark windshield and a chrome plated turbine in the back. There can be different shades of this car. The Terrible Turbo is a derivative of the Turbo Turn On car. It is a molded one piece body. The turbo on the rear is chrome plated. The car is on a magna-steering chassis and was used in the battery operated Scre-e-echers Sets. The car was produced as a Scre-e-echer until 1977 and then re-issued in 1982 as a Lazer 2000 with the turbo removed and the mold modified. The Spider Mobile is the Terrible Turbo car. It is a molded one piece body. The turbo on the rear is chrome plated. The car is on a magna-steering fixed pin chassis and was used in the battery operated Scre-e-echers Sets.

#	Description		Rating	Color
1755	non-magnatraction	☐	-4-	yellow/blue
		☐	-3-	orange/purple/yellow
5787	magna-steering	☐	-4-	blue/red/white
5807	magna-steering pin	☐	-3-	blue/red/white with stars (different sizes)
2012	Odyssey 2000	☐	-3-	white/red/pink/light red
2013	Starfire 2000	☐	-3-	white/light blue/dark blue
5811	magna-steering pin	☐	-4-	blue/red/white Spiderman

Grand Am Funny Car 1974-78

The Grand Am featured the specialty chassis and had mag wheels and wide rear tires. The windshield is tinted red and the rear bumper is a chrome plated separate piece with (2) wheelie bars. A front screw holds the chassis to the body.

#	Description		Rating	Color
1702	non-magnatraction	☐	-5-	white/red/blue
1926	magnatraction	☐	-5-	white/red/blue
		☐	-4-	yellow/orange
		☐	-1-	blue/yellow/red

Plymouth "Cuda" Funny Car 1971-74

The "Cuda" Funny Car is a one piece molded body with a tinted windshield with the letters "CUDA" etched in it or they can be cut out. The rear wheelie bar is a separate chrome plated piece and is usually missing or broken. The front wheels and axle are mounted to the body due to the length of the car.

1758	non-magnatraction	☐ -4-	orange/purple/yellow
		☐ -4-	white/red/blue
		☐ -4-	white/blue/red
		☐ -1-	blue/white
		☐ -5-	white/red/yellow
		☐ -4-	white/orange/mustard
		☐ -4-	white/red

Pinto Funny Car 1972-74

The Pinto Funny Car is a one piece molded body with a tinted windshield with the letters Pinto etched on the front spoiler. The rear wheelie bar is a separate chrome plated piece and is usually missing or broken. The front wheels and axle are mounted to the body due to the length of the car. This car can vary in shades.

1761	non-magnatraction	☐ -5-	lime green/blue
		☐ -4-	orange/purple
		☐ -3-	blue/white
		☐ -3-	white/red flames

'71 Vega Van Gasser 1971-74

The Vega is a one piece molded body with a tinted windshield. The rear wheelie bar is a separate chrome plated piece and is usually missing or broken. The front wheels and axle are mounted to the body due to the length of the car.

1759　non-magnatraction　　☐ -5-　yellow/red flames
　　　　　　　　　　　　　　☐ -3-　translucent yellow/red flames
　　　　　　　　　　　　　　☐ -1-　yellow
　　　　　　　　　　　　　　☐ -1-　orange
　　　　　　　　　　　　　　☐ -3-　white/flourescent flames
　　　　　　　　　　　　　　☐ -3-　orange/red flames

Porsche 917 1971-78

The Porsche is a one piece molded body with clear headlight lenses and they can have a clear or black windshield. There can be open or closed air vents in the front. The number can be heavy or light print.

1757　non-magnatraction　　　☐ -4-　light blue/orange #2
1902　magnatraction　　　　　☐ -4-　light blue/orange #2
1798　non-magna. lighted　　　☐ -4-　light blue/orange #2
1973　magnatraction lighted　 ☐ -4-　light blue/orange #2
　　　　　　　　　　　　　　☐ -5-　white/green/yellow #2
　　　　　　　　　　　　　　☐ -3-　white/purple #2
　　　　　　　　　　　　　　☐ -5-　yellow/blue #2
　　　　　　　　　　　　　　☐ -1-　white/blue #2

Ferrari 512M 1972-78

The Ferrari is a one piece molded body with clear headlight lenses and a clear or darkened windshield. The rear spoiler is a separate piece along with the motor in back. This car comes with or without the open air vent in the front.

1763	non-magnatraction	☐ -5-	blue/yellow #6
		☐ -5-	red/white #6
1905	magnatraction	☐ -5-	red/white #6
		☐ -5-	red/white #2
1799	non-magna.lighted	☐ -4-	blue/yellow #6
1974	magnatraction lighted	☐ -4-	dark blue/yellow #6
		☐ -4-	blue/white #2
		☐ -5-	white/blue #6
		☐ -5-	white/blue #2
		☐ -1-	red/yellow #211

AFX Super II 1972-73

The world's fastest HO scale production car, so Aurora claimed. The car featured a bullet proof Quadra-lam armature capable of over 60,000 RPM. It was a light weight vacuum formed body with hinged body mount integrated into the front nose weight. The chassis also had side weights. Braided pickups and super trued rear tires were featured along with small "O" ring front tires on aluminum turned hubs. There is a Bell helmeted driver and chrome plated engine intake behind him. The Quadra-lam armature (black) is desirable today. The car and chassis come in a blue and silver velvet lined presentation box. A red/white/blue version and a blue version were never made.

1788-880	non-magnatraction	☐ -2-	yellow/black #4
-881	non-magnatraction	☐ -2-	red/black #4

Corvette "A" Production 1974-78

The "A" Corvette is a one piece molded body with a windshield. Several variations are shown and they are extremely limited in production. Side pipes can be white or silver. Grills are painted black or non painted.

1703	non-magnatraction	☐	-4-	yellow/black/white side pipes
1927	magnatraction	☐	-4-	yellow/black/silver side pipes
		☐	-4-	white/blue/red/silver #7
		☐	-3-	chrome/light blue
		☐	-3-	chrome/red
		☐	-3-	black/yellow
		☐	-3-	dark blue/white

☐	-1-	white/orng	-1- ☐	white/lime	-1- ☐	white/purple
☐	-1-	white/blue	-1- ☐	blue/blue	-1- ☐	blue/green
☐	-1-	blue/white	-1- ☐	gold	-1- ☐	orange/yellow
☐	-1-	orange/wht	-1- ☐	orange/red	-1- ☐	red/orange
☐	-1-	red/white	-1- ☐	yellow/red	-1- ☐	yellow/orange

Corvette Funny Car 1972-74

The Corvette is a one piece molded body with a chrome plated blower motor and chrome plated driver inside. The rear wheelie bar and bumper is a separate piece and is usually missing or broken. The front bumper is chrome plated. The front wheels and axle are mounted to the body due to the length of the car.

1766   non-magnatraction   ☐ -4-   white/red/blue
                                     ☐ -3-   orange/purple
                                     ☐ -2-   yellow/black

Corvette GT 1979-81

The Corvette GT body is a one piece molded one with a separate rear bumper. The windshield is tinted. The car has provisions for the lighted feature.

6202	**Speed Steer**	☐ -3-	white/light blue/dark blue #6
1954	**magnatraction**	☐ -5-	orange/red/silver #12
1982	**magnatraction lighted**	☐ -5-	orange/red/silver #12
1980		☐ -5-	yellow/blue #12
1011	**Blazin Brakes**	☐ -3-	white/yellow/orange/red #3
1022	**Cats Eyes**	☐ -5-	yellow/blue #12

Vega Funny Car 1976-79

The Funny Vega is a one piece molded body with chrome plated separate bumpers front and rear. There is a chrome plated blower in front and the windshield glass is tinted. The rear has a high spoiler which is often broken. The car rides on the magnatraction specialty chassis. Some variations are silver on the rear and front spoilers.

1934   magnatraction   ☐ -4-   white/orange/blue
                                 ☐ -4-   orange/white/red

"Dodge Fever" 1973-76
"Furious Fueler" 1973-76
"Aztec" 1973-76
"Dyno-Mite" 1973-76

The Dodge is the first ever, HO dragster. It was designed to drag race on straight AFX high performance track. It features the specialty chassis with a dragster extended front end plus super wide super size rear sponge tires. It came with it's own custom decals and was packaged in a bubble pack. There is a wire to the front wheels and front chrome plated bumper and a chrome plated rear with twin chutes and wheelie bars. The bars are often broken off. The windshield is tinted blue.

The "Fueler" was designed to drag race on straight AFX high performance track. It features the specialty chassis with a dragster extended front end plus super wide super size rear sponge tires. It came with it's own custom decals and was packaged in a bubble pack. There is a wire to the front wheels and chrome plated driver and engine, along with a chrome plated rear with wheelie bars. The bars are often broken off.

The Aztec is the same body style as the Dodge (#1772). It was designed to drag race on straight AFX high performance track. It features the specialty chassis with a dragster extended front end plus super wide super size rear sponge tires. It came with it's own custom decals and was packaged in a bubble pack. There is a wire to the front wheels and front chrome plated bumper and a chrome plated rear with twin chutes and wheelie bars. The bars are often broken off. The windshield is tinted blue.

The Dyno was designed to drag race on straight AFX high performance track. It features the specialty chassis with a dragster extended front end plus super wide super size rear sponge tires. It came with it's own custom decals and was packaged in a bubble pack. There is a wire to the front wheels and chrome plated driver and motor and a chrome plated rear with wheelie bars. The bars are often broken.

1772	non-magnatraction	☐ -3-	white/yellow
1961	magnatraction	☐ -3-	white/yellow
1774	non-magnatraction	☐ -3-	white/yellow
1962	magnatraction	☐ -3-	white/yellow
1792	non-magnatraction	☐ -3-	candy plated red
1963	magnatraction	☐ -3-	candy plated red
1794	non-magnatraction	☐ -3-	white/light blue
1964	magnatraction	☐ -3-	white/light blue

Daytona Charger 1971-79

The Charger is a one piece molded body with a fragile wing molded in. There is a full windshield. Some versions come with the #7 outlined in silver. In 1976 provisions for a flamethrower body were made and the car mold was modified. There are different shades of this car. It can come with or without silver trim around the number 7. The hood has been seen in both gloss and flat finish. /the gloss being the harder of the two.

1753	non-magnatraction	☐ -4-	orange/black #7
		☐ -4-	blue/black #7
		☐ -1-	dark blue/black #7
1900	magnatraction	☐ -4-	blue/black #7
	lighted magnatraction	☐ -5-	yellow/black #7 (no trim)
		☐ -4-	blue/black #7 (no trim)

Dodge Charger Stock Car 1972-78

The Charger is a one piece molded body with chrome plated bumpers front and rear along with a tinted windshield. The hood is flat black.

1773	non-magnatraction	☐ -4-	white/black red #11
		☐ -4-	yellow/black red #11
1910	magnatraction	☐ -4-	yellow/black, red #11
		☐ -3-	lime/black blue #11
		☐ -3-	lime/black red #11
		☐ -1-	plated gold
		☐ -1-	plated copper
		☐ -1-	orange/red/blue #11 w/flag (Rebel Charger)
1063	magna-sonic	☐ -4-	mustard/black red #11
1101	Super magnatraction	☐ -4-	gold chrome/blue red #11
		☐ -1-	blue/red/white #43 w/stickers (TV Guide promo)

Plymouth Road Runner Stock Car 1972-79

The Road Runner is a one piece molded body with a separate front and rear bumper. The rear is chrome plated and the front is painted. There is a windshield and the car comes in both two tone and solid colors.

1762	non-magnatraction	☐ -4-	blue/white #43
1904	magnatraction	☐ -4-	blue/white #43
		☐ -2-	blue/red #43 (red nose)
		☐ -2-	blue/red #43 (blue nose)
		☐ -2-	yellow #43
		☐ -1-	red #43
		☐ -4-	white/blue #43
		☐ -5-	yellow/orange #43
1062	magna-sonic	☐ -5-	orange/yellow orange #30
		☐ -4-	orange/yellow brown #30
		☐ -4-	right blue/dark blue #30
		☐ -4-	red/blue #43

Chevelle Stocker 1974-79

The Chevelle is a one piece body and has a separate chrome plated front and rear bumper. There is a full tinted windshield. The # 427 is across the hood. In 1976 the body mold was modified to accept the flamethrower chassis.

Continued on next page.

109

Chevelle Stocker 1974-79 (continued)

1929	magnatraction	☐ -5-	white/orange #17
1975	lighted magnatraction	☐ -5-	white/orange #17
		☐ -4-	yellow/red #17
		☐ -3-	orange/white #17
		☐ -1-	blue/lime green #17
1067	magna-sonic	☐ -3-	red/white/orange #29
		☐ -4-	white/red/blue #29

Javelin Trans AM 1972-79
Javelin Pro Stocker 1972-74

The Javelin is a one piece molded body with separate front and rear chrome plated bumpers. The windshield is tinted and the hood is the only difference between this car and the Pro Stocker version. The Javelin is a one piece molded body with separate front and rear chrome plated bumpers. The windshield is tinted and the hood is the only difference between this car and the Trans Am version.

1764	non-magnatraction	☐ -4-	white/red/blue #6
1906	magnatraction	☐ -4-	white/red/blue #6
		☐ -4-	mustard/red silver #5
		☐ -4-	chrome/red blue #5
		☐ -4-	mustard/red black #5
1069	magna-sonic	☐ -3-	blue/light blue/black #21
		☐ -4-	red/white #5
		☐ -5-	blue/black #5
		☐ -2-	white/yellow/orange #21
1765	non-magnatraction	☐ -3-	yellow/black (Pro Stock)
		☐ -1-	white/violet (Pro Stock)
		☐ -2-	orange/black (Pro Stock)
		☐ -2-	lime/black (Pro Stock)

Matador Stock Car 1973-78

This car is a one piece molded body with chrome plated bumpers front and rear. There is a full windshield.

1787	non-magnatraction	☐ -3-	white/red/blue #16
1916	magnatraction	☐ -3-	white/red/blue #16
		☐ -4-	white/blue #2
3005	ultra 5	☐ -4-	yellow/red #2

Matador Stock 1975-77

The Matador is a one piece molded body with a tinted windshield. There are separate chrome plated bumpers front and rear. The #425 or #355 is across the hood.

1930	magnatraction	☐ -5-	white/blue/red #5
		☐ -4-	orange/red/black #5
		☐ -4-	white/yellow/red #1
		☐ -2-	white/blue #5

Matador Taxi 1976-77
Matador Police Vehicle 1976-78

The Matador Taxi replaced the stocker #1787. There is a chrome plated taxi sign bar on top. There are (3) paper stickers on the sides and trunk. A neat scuff mark or two depicts a real taxi. The Matador Police also replaced the stocker #1787. There is a chrome plated light and siren bar on top.

1938	magnatraction	☐ -5-	white/black #2-C5
	magnatraction	☐ -5-	blue/white/black #2-C5
1939	magnatraction	☐ -4-	white/black
		☐ -4-	yellow/black
		☐ -3-	light blue/black

'56 Ford Pickup 1976-79
Fall Guy Pick Up Truck 1982

The '56 Ford is a popular vehicle. It is a one piece molded body with a separate chrome plated front bumper. There are (2) chrome plated exhaust stacks on the sides. These are frequently broken or missing. The flamed paint job sets off the truck. It sits angled on a specialty chassis. The Fall Guy is the first of the Aurora licenced products. It is a one piece molded body with a separate front and rear chrome plated bumper. The front has an additional chrome winch and the light and roll bar in the bed is also chrome plated. The designers made a mistake and molded the body to tight and it is quite difficult to remove the chassis.

1941	magnatraction	☐ -3-	black/tan with red/yellow flames
		☐ -3-	red/black with blue/white flames
1971	magnatraction	☐ -3-	brown/tan w/(3) Fall Guy stickers

Dodge Magnum Stock Car 1979-83

The Magnum is a one piece molded body with a full tinted windshield. There are chrome plated bumpers front and rear. The #360 engine size is across the hood.

1073	Magna-Sonic	☐ -4-	butterscotch/wine/black #8
6205	Speed Steer	☐ -5-	white/red/orange #14
1959	magnatraction	☐ -4-	blue/light blue/white #8
		☐ -5-	white/red/orange #14
2805	super G-plus	☐ -0-	white/blue/red/orange #14

Thunderbird Stock Car 1979-83

The T'bird Stocker is a one piece molded body with a full tinted windshield. There are chrome plated bumpers front and rear. The #351 engine size is across the hood.

1074	Magna-Sonic	☐ -4-	white/blue #12
1956	magnatraction	☐ -4-	white/blue #12
		☐ -3-	red/orange #12
		☐ -5-	white/blue/yellow/green #20
6204	Speed Steer	☐ -5-	white/blue/yellow/green #20
2804	Super G-Plus	☐ -0-	white/red/orange/yellow #20 (not shown)

Mercury Stocker 1975-82

The Mercury has the #1707 molded inside the one piece body. This was probably originally going to be released as a non-magnatraction car. There is a full tinted windshield and chrome plated bumpers front and rear. The # 429 or #351 is across the hood.

1932	magnatraction	☐ -4-	white/black/gold #31
		☐ -4-	light blue/white #31
1951		☐ -5-	plated purple #17 (different shades)
3006	ultra 5	☐ -3-	white/red/blue #2 (Union stickers)
6290	Speed Steer	☐ -5-	plated purple #17 (road blocker) (diff. shades)

'57 Corvette Hardtop 1981-82
'57 Corvette Convertible 1981-82

The '57 Vette is a popular car today. It is a one piece molded body that was used for both the convertible and hardtop versions. The number molded inside is that of the convertible. There is a separate front chrome plated shark's tooth grill. The hood is a separate smooth piece. There is a tinted windshield and top molded in one piece and mask sprayed. The Vette convertible has a separate front chrome plated diamond plate grill. The hood is a separate piece with two carbs showing. There is a tinted windshield and a chrome plated roll bar attached.

1968	magnatraction	☐ -2-	red/white
1969	magnatraction	☐ -2-	yellow/orange/red

'55 Chevy Bel Air 1973-79

The '55 Chevy is a very popular model. It is a one piece molded body with a tinted windshield and a hood scoop to match. The front bumper is chrome plated and the back one is also. On the back bumper are (2) shackles that are underneath where the chassis fits the body. These are often missing or broken. There are molded in side pipes beneath the doors and these are frequently broken also. The tail lights can come with or without detailing.

1777	non-magnatraction	☐	-4-	lime green/white pipes
1913	magnatraction	☐	-4-	lime green/white pipes
		☐	-3-	translucent yellow/white pipes
		☐	-5-	yellow/silver pipes
		☐	-5-	yellow/white pipes
		☐	-2-	yellow/white pipes w/stickers (Rat 55 Set Car)
1108	super magnatraction	☐	-3-	gold chrome #28 (6) stickers
		☐	-1-	red chrome #28
		☐	-3-	copper chrome #28 (different shades)
1064	magna-sonic	☐	-2-	black/yellow flames
		☐	-2-	white/red flames
		☐	-4-	blue/silver pipes

'57 Chevy Nomad 1971-81

The Nomad is a one piece molded body that has a full tinted windshield and chrome plated bumpers front and rear. The side pipes came in white, silver, orange, blue. There are many shade variations on the Nomad. This car was and is, so popular, that it is still being manufactured today.

Continued on next page.

'57 Chevy Nomad 1971-81 (continued)

1760	non-magnatraction	☐ -5-	pink/white side pipes
		☐ -5-	pink/silver side pipes
1903	magnatraction	☐ -5-	pink/white side pipes
		☐ -5-	orange/white side pipes
		☐ -5-	orange/blue side pipes
		☐ -3-	yellow/silver side pipes
		☐ -3-	yellow/oange side pipes
		☐ -4-	blue/white side pipes
		☐ -1-	white/silver side pipes
		☐ -1-	brown/white side pipes
		☐ -1-	orange/yellow starburst
		☐ -2-	pink/burgundy stripes
		☐ -2-	green/metallic green stripes
		☐ -2-	blue/silver stripes
		☐ -1-	red/white starburst
1991	SP Fast	☐ -4-	purple chrome #21
		☐ -2-	blue chrome #21
		☐ -1-	silver chrome #21

Bre Datsun 240Z 1973-80
Continued on next page.

Bre Datsun 240Z 1973-80 (continued)

The 240Z is a one piece molded body with a chrome plated front and rear bumper. There is a windshield.

1775	non-magnatraction	☐ -5-	red/white/blue #46
1911	magnatraction	☐ -5-	red/white/blue #46
		☐ -4-	white/green w/white stripes #46
		☐ -4-	white/green w/yellow stripes #46
		☐ -1-	red/white/blue w/stickers (Polaroid promo Set)
1739	G-Plus	☐ -4-	red/orange/white #17 paper stickers
1104	Super magnatraction	☐ -4-	plated chrome/light blue #46
1990	SP Fast	☐ -4-	plated chrome/light blue #46

Bre Datsun 510 "Trans Am" 1973-78

The 510 is a one piece molded body with a chrome plated bumper front and rear. The rear one is a small bar that goes straight across. There is a full windshield that is tinted blue. The windshield posts are fragile. There is a very exclusive Datsun that was offered as a mail in with Sugar Daddy candy. It is very hard to find today.

1776	non-magnatraction	☐ -5-	red/white/blue #46
1912	magnatraction	☐ -4-	red/white/blue #35
		☐ -1-	olive drab metal flake #166 w/stickers (Sugar Daddy)
		☐ -1-	dark olive metal flake #166 w/stickers (Sugar Daddy)
		☐ -4-	dark blue/white #35
		☐ -3-	medium blue/white #35
		☐ -4-	light blue/white #35
1071	magna-sonic	☐ -5-	yellow/orange #46

Datsun Baja Pick Up 1974-82

Continued on next page.

Datsun Baja Pick Up 1974-82 *(continued)*

The Datsun Pick Up is a one piece molded body with a blue tinted windshield. There is a chrome plated roll bar as well as a chrome plated front bumper. There are different shades of each color and they can come with or without the #211. A set was made exclusively for Polaroid employees and the truck with the correct stickers is very desirable.

745	non-magnatraction	☐ -5-	yellow/black #211
1919	magnatraction	☐ -5-	yellow/black #211
		☐ -1-	yellow/black w/Polaroid Stickers
		☐ -4-	blue/black w/ or w/o the #211
		☐ -4-	mustard/black w/ or w/o the #211

Ford Baja Bronco 1972-77

The Bronco is an off road vehicle. It is a one piece body with a separate chrome plated front bumper and top. The front grille and push bar can be detailed or plain. There are (2) drivers inside, both with Bell helmets. There is a painted spare tire molded in back.

1769	non-magnatraction	☐ -5-	yellow/white/black #3
		☐ -4-	red/white/black #3
		☐ -3-	translucent yellow/white/black #3
1909	magnatraction	☐ -4-	red/white/black #l3
		☐ -4-	bue/white/black #3

"Baja Bug" VW 1973-78

The Baja Bug is a one piece molded body with accented gas tanks molded in the sides. Thee is a useable spare tire on top. The front bumper is chrome plated with (5) lights (3 up and 2 down) on a bar. The rear has a chrome plated exhaust and engine. There can be varying shades of this car. *Continued on next page.*

"Baja Bug" VW 1973-78 (continued)

1778	non-magnatraction	☐ -4-	yellow/black tanks
1914	magnatraction	☐ -4-	yellow/black tanks
		☐ -3-	translucent yellow/blue tanks
		☐ -2-	white/black tanks
		☐ -5-	green/blue tanks
1065	magna-sonic	☐ -4-	red/white tanks
		☐ -1-	red/black tanks

Roarin' Rolls "Golden Ghost" 1973-77

The Rolls is a one piece molded body and is the first car to use the new specially modified AFX chassis. The chassis has super size rear whels and tires, along with a four gear drive train arrangement. The front grill is gold plated with a winged "golden ghost" on it. The wings are frequently broken. The rear has a gold plated bumper, twin parachutes, and a single wheelie bar and wheel. The wheelie bar is almost always broken or missing.

1781	non-magnatraction	☐ -4-	white/black
1923	magnatraction	☐ -4-	white/black
		☐ -4-	black/white
		☐ -4-	yellow/black
		☐ -3-	translucent yellow/black

Peace Tank 1973-77

The Peace Tank was Aurora's way of condemning the U. S. involvement in the Vietnam conflict of the early 70's. The young designers made a one piece molded body with loads of goodies on it. A separate turret with a chrome plated gun barrel tied in a knot. Push it down and a large nosed soldier with a chrome plated helmet pops up. There is a separate rear wing and a chrome plated engine with two bent exhaust pipes. There is a guitar molded in front and a beer can behind the driver. Look for the DPW manhole under the turret. This car uses the specialty chassis.

1782	non-magnatraction	☐ -5-	olive drab/yellow
		☐ -5-	light olive drab/yellow
1924	magnatraction	☐ -5-	olive drab/yellow

Lola T-330 1976-80

The Lola is a one piece molded body with a separate chrome plated wing. There are (2) mirrors and a blower on the motor. The cockpit surround is chrome plated as are the (2) exhaust pipes. There are paper stickers on the front, sides, and rear wing for a total of (6). The International set provides a plain car and allows you to decal up to 18 different countries.

1731	G-Plus	☐ -4-	white/blue #7
		☐ -5-	yellow/red #7
		☐ -3-	red/white
		☐ -3-	light blue/dark blue
1716	Super G-Plus	☐ -4-	chrome/orange #7
		☐ -1-	white/blue International Set (18 countries)

Ferrari 312 PB 1976-79
Ferrari F1 1976-79

The Ferrari is a one piece molded body with a molded wing. There are (2) mirrors and a blower on the motor. There is a black roll bar behind the driver There are paper stickers on the front and sides for a total of (4). The F1 Ferrari is a one piece molded body with a separate two piece wing and base. There are (2) mirrors and a blower on the motor. The cockpit surround is tinted. There are paper stickers on the front, sides, and rear wing for a total of (8).

German Faller packaging

1734	G-Plus	☐ -5-	red/white #6
1732	G-Plus	☐ -4-	red/yellow/white #2

McLaren F1 1976-83

The McLaren is a one piece molded body with a separate wing. There are (2) mirrors and a blower on the motor. The cockpit windshield is tinted. There are paper stickers on the front, top, sides, and rear wing for a total of (13).

1733	G-Plus	☐ -4-	red/white #11
1745		☐ -3-	yellow/blue Aurora #1 w/scoop, Tiger, Solo
		☐ -3-	yellow/blue Aurora #1 w/scoop, no tiger or Solo
1829	G-Plus	☐ -3-	yellow/blue Aurora #1 w/Tiger, Solo, no scoop
		☐ -5-	white/flourescent pink #11
2845	Super G-Plus	☐ -3-	yellow/blue Aurora Tiger #1

Indy Special 1976-80

The Indy is a one piece molded body with a separate wing and base. There are (2) mirrors. The cockpit surround is clear and the (2) exhaust pipes are chrome plated. There are paper stickers on the front, sides, and top for a total of (5).

1735	G-Plus	☐ -4-	black/red/orange/yellow/white #1
1789		☐ -4-	orange (Foyt Indy) #14 w/stickers
		☐ -3-	orange (Foyt Indy) #14 w/stencils
		☐ -4-	white/red/orange/yellow #1
1796		☐ -1-	red/orange/yellow/white #16
1715	Super G-Plus	☐ -4-	gold/red/orange/yellow/white #1

Ferrari Daytona Coupe 1976-81

The Ferrari Daytona is a one piece molded body with a separate front and rear lower bumper added on. There are (2) mirrors and the windshield is tinted. There are paper or masked #'s on the doors. Some of the cars can be found with detailing on the rear lights.

1736	G-Plus	☐ -5-	yellow/green/black #16 w/stickers
1964	magnatraction	☐ -3-	red #16
1992	SP Fast	☐ -5-	yellow/green/black #16
		☐ -4-	yellow/green/black #16 w/stencils

6 Wheel Elf 1977-80
Formula 5000 1980-82

The Elf is a one piece molded body with a few different intake variations. The rear spoiler is a separate piece and the front air dam can be louvered or solid. There are (9) paper stickers on the car. This car can be stenciled or have stickers. There are versions with and without the scoop behind the driver. There is a variation with an added cross piece on the rear spoiler. The following description is for the Formula 5000 series. These cars were produced in Europe by Faller/Aurora for the foreign market. The body is similar to the 6 wheel Elf with the front modified to eliminate the extra wheels.

1738	G-Plus	☐ -4-	blue #4
1791		☐ -2-	blue #4 w/Citibank stickers
1835	F-5000 G-Plus	☐ -1-	blue/yellow #1 Citizens Watch
1792	(5636) F-5000	☐ -1-	white/blue/purple/red #8 Polifac (Faller/Aurora)
5635	F-5000	☐ -1-	black/yellow #1 AMS Racing (Faller/Aurora)

Ferrari T4 Formula 1 1980
Ligier Formula 1 1980

The Ferrari has no number molded in the one piece body. There is a separate cockpit tinted windshield. The rear low wing is a separate piece also. There are (8) paper stickers on the car. The Ligier is a one piece molded body and wing configuration. There are (3) paper stickers on it.

1740	G-Plus	-4-	red/silver #2
1802	Speed Shifter	-4-	red/silver #2
1785	G-Plus	-3-	blue/white/red stripe #26

Lotus '79 F1 1979-83

The Lotus is a one piece molded body with a separate piece high wing on back. There are a total of (10) paper stickers on it.

1783	G-Plus	-5-	black #1
1718		-2-	yellow/black Madom #3
1793		-2-	dark blue Essex Tissot (silver stickers)
1794		-3-	red/blue Candy Tyrell
2883	Super G-Plus	-5-	black #1
2893		-1-	dark blue Essex Tissot (paper stickers)
2894		-3-	red/blue Candy Tyrell

Williams Formula 1 1980-83
Renault Formula 1 1980-83

The Williams repeats the #1787. It is a one piece molded body with a separate piece rear wing. There are (8) paper stickers on the car. The Renault is a one piece molded body and there is no number molded in. The car has a molded in rear wrap around wing. There are (10) paper stickers on the car.

1787	G-Plus	☐ -3-	white/green #1 Saudia
1836		☐ -2-	white/blue #8 Bata Din
		☐ -1-	fourescent #7 Watson
2887	Super G-Plus	☐ -3-	white/green #1 Saudia
1801	Speed Shifter	☐ -3-	white/green #1 Saudia
1788	G-Plus	☐ -4-	yellow/white #15
		☐ -3-	translucent yellow/white #15
2888	Super G-Plus	☐ -4-	yellow/white #15

Model 'A' Ford Panel 1973-77

The Panel truck is a one piece molded body with a black painted roof. The full windshield is tinted blue and the front headlights and grill are chrome plated. The fenders are a separate piece molded in black. The car rides on the specialty chassis.

1791	non-magnatraction	☐ -4-	lime
1925	magnatraction	☐ -1-	orange
		☐ -4-	mustard
		☐ -3-	black

Model "A" 1930 Ford Coupe 1974-77
'29 Model "A" Woodie 1974-77

The coupe is a one piece molded body that has the same black fenders as #1791. There is a windshield and the front radiator and lights are a separate chrome plated piece. The Woodie is a one piece molded body that sits on a separate black molded fender piece that is identical to #1791. The front radiator and headlights are chrome plated. The car rides on the specialty chassis and is held in place by a screw.

1928	magnatraction	☐ -4-	yellow
		☐ -2-	black
		☐ -3-	blue
1746	non-magnatraction	☐ -5-	butterscotch/brown/black
1920	magnatraction	☐ -5-	butterscotch/brown/black

VW Thing Roadster 1976-77
VW Thing 1975-77

The VW Thing is The same body as #1931. It has a flip down front clear plastic windshield. Thee is a separate roll bar and convertible top (folded down) on the rear deck. The car has a Bell helmeted driver and rides on the specialty chassis. The Thing was an interesting car of the day. The real one was based on '40's German staff cars. Aurora made a one piece molded body with a Bell helmeted driver inside. The rear deck is a separate piece molded in the same color as the body. The top is clear plastic and is sprayed white or black to simulate a convertible top up. It rides on the specialty chassis and is held in place by a screw.

1936	magnatraction	-4-	brown/tan camouflage
		-4-	lime/green camouflage
1931	magnatraction	-5-	blue/white top
		-5-	yellow/black top

Monza GT 1978-81

The Monza is a one piece molded body with a separate piece for the rear bumper. There is a full windshield. There is a wing on back and the body is set up to be a flamethrower.

1948	magnatrction	-5-	red/yellow #0
		-1-	black/yellow/orange/red #25
1977	lighted magnatraction	-5-	red/yellow #0
		-4-	white/green #0
1012	blazin brakes	-4-	white/blue/red/orange #5

Porsche 934 Turbo 1979-81

The Porsche Turbo is a one piece molded body with a tinted windshield. There is a large "whale tail" spoiler on back which is frequently found broken or missing. There is a silver paper "Turbo RSR" sticker on the windshield.

1955	magnatraction	☐ -5-	yellow/orange/red #51
		☐ -4-	black/burgundy/white #51
6203	Speed Steer	☐ -4-	white/orange #81
		☐ -1-	yellow/black #81
		☐ -5-	yellow/orange/red #51
1781	G-Plus	☐ -1-	yellow/brown/orange #31
1804	speed shifter	☐ -4-	red/white/yellow/orange #7
1013	blazin brakes	☐ -4-	red/white/yellow/orange #7

Porsche Carrera 1975-82

The Carrera is a one piece molded body with a separate rear panel below the wing. This was to prevent a molding problem called lock-on from occuring. That is when a part is locked on to the mold after forming due to the design. There is a full tinted windshield. Some versions of this car have silver headlights.

| 1933 | magnatraction | ☐ -4- | white/purple/black #3 |
| | magnatraction | ☐ -4- | orange/blue/black #3 |

BMW 320i Turbo 1979-82

The BMW 320i is a one piece molded body with a separate front and rear bumper attached. There is a high rear spoiler and the windshield is tinted. There are (3) silver paper stickers on it. Provisions are made inside for the lighted feature.

1980	magnatraction lighted	☐ -5-	white/red/blue #3
		☐ -3-	white/red/blue (#3 on roof)
		☐ -2-	red/blue/white #9
6201	Speed Steer	☐ -5-	yellow/orange #5
		☐ -5-	yellow/red/orange #3
		☐ -5-	yellow/orange/red #3

BMW M1 1980-81

The BMW M1 is a one piece molded body with a tinted windshield.

1957	magnatraction	☐ -4-	white/red/blue #3
		☐ -4-	white/blue/red #11
1803	Speed Shifter	☐ -4-	white/red/blue #3
1993	SP Fast	☐ -2-	white/red/black #9 (4) Valvoline stickers

Ford Escort 1976-82

The Ford Escort is a one piece molded body with a separate front and rear bumper added on. The front one is mask sprayed on the bottom air dam to match the car. The windshield is tinted. There are (6) paper decals on the sides, hood, and trunk of the car.

Continued on next page.

Ford Escort 1976-82 (continued)

1944	G-Plus	-3-	white/red/blue (#46 in red)
		-3-	white/red/blue (#46 in silver)
1103	super magnatraction	-4-	gold chrome/blue/red #46
1072	magna-sonic	-4-	light blue/dark blue/white #46
6291	Speed Steer	-3-	white/red/blue #46 (road blocker)
		-5-	plated purple #21
1951	magnatraction	-5-	plated copper #21
		-5-	plated gold #21
		-2-	black/red/green #46

Capri Funny Car 1976-81

The Capri is a one piece molded body with a chrome plated front grille insert and a separate piece front valance. The windshield is tinted. The number 13 can be present on the hood or not. There is an International Capri made by Aurora and Faller for Aurora which were both marketed in Europe. They come with stickers to allow for different nation detailing.

1935	magnatraction	-4-	white/black/blue #13
		-4-	orange/burgundy/white #13
1742	G-Plus	-4-	white/blue/green #21 paper stickers
		-2-	International Set
		-2-	International Faller Set
1994	SP Fast	-1-	white/green/red Alitalia (4) stickers

Rallye Ford Escort 1976-81

The Rallye Ford a one piece molded body with a separate front and rear bumper added on. The front one is mask sprayed on the bottom air dam to match the car and it also has a light bar on it. There are (2) tires on a rack on top and the windshield is tinted. There are (9) paper decals on the sides, hood, and trunk of the car.

1737	G-Plus	☐ -3-	lime/blue #28 w/stickers
		☐ -5-	lime/blue #28 w/stencils
1997	SP Fast	☐ -2-	white/blue/yellow/red Castrol (5) stickers

Dodge Street Van 1974-79

The Dodge Van is a one piece molded body with a tinted full windshield. There is a separate chrome bumper on the front and rear. The rear one is often missing. The car rides on the specialty chassis and is held on by a screw.

1748	non-magnatraction	☐ -5-	yellow/orange stripe
1922	magnatraction	☐ -5-	lime green/blue stripe
		☐ -5-	orange/black
		☐ -4-	orange/no stripe

Custom Van 1976-79

The Custom Van is a one piece molded body with a separate chrome plated front grill that has the bottom air dam mask sprayed the color of the van. There is a tinted windshield and the phrase "keep on truckin" is stenciled on back. The van rides on the specialty chassis.

1942	magnatraction	☐ -4-	orange/black/red
		☐ -4-	white/black/light blue
		☐ -3-	orange/black/purple

Ford Street Van 1976-82

The Ford Van is a one piece molded body. It has a separate chrome plated bumper in the front and rear. The windshield is tinted. This van rides on the specialty chassis.

1943	magnatraction	☐ -4-	white/blue
		☐ -2-	black
		☐ -4-	tan/brown

Dodge Van Rescue Vehicle 1976-78
Police Van 1978-79

The Dodge Van Rescue is on the same body as #1922. There is a separate cap on top with (4) rescue lights on it. They are not illuminated. The van says EUCSER on the front like a real rescue van would. It rides on the specialty chassis. The Police van is the same body as the #1748 Street Van. It has a top on it with (4) non-functional lights. It rides on the specialty chassis.

1937	magnatraction	☐ -5-	white/orange
		☐ -5-	red/white
1946	magnatraction	☐ -5-	white/black #1-226
		☐ -5-	blue/black/white #1-226

Blazer 1980-82

The Blazer is a one piece molded body with separate front and rear chrome plated bumpers. There is a tinted window and there are provisions for the lighted feature.

1959	magnatraction	☐ -4-	white/red/orange/yellow
1917		☐	
1984	magnatraction lighted	☐ -4-	black/dark blue/light blue/white
6206	speed steer	☐ -4-	white/red/orange/yellow
1020	cats eyes	☐ -2-	white with red/orange flames

Jeep CJ-7 1980

The Jeep is a one piece molded body with a fragile front bumper. It has a tinted window and there are provisions for the lighted feature

1962	magnatraction	☐ -5-	light blue/dark blue/black
1918		☐	
1987	magnatraction lighted	☐ -5-	red/yellow/black
6207	speed steer	☐ -3-	yellow/orange/black (4x4)
1021	cats eyes	☐ -5-	red/yellow/black

Trans Am Camaro Z28 1971-79

The Camaro is a one piece molded body with a fragile rear chrome plated bumper. The windshield is clear. Later the body was modified for a flamethrower lighted car. There can be different shades of this car.

1756	non- magnatraction	☐ -4-	white/blue #3
		☐ -4-	light blue/purple #3
1901	magnatraction	☐ -4-	light blue/purple #3
		☐ -4-	white/blue/red/silver #6
		☐ -1-	white/orange #3
1978	lighted magnatraction	☐ -4-	white/blue/red/silver #6
		☐ -4-	light blue/purple #3
1023	cats eyes	☐ -4-	white/blue/red/silver #6

Firebird 1979-82

The Firebird is a one piece molded body in a "T" top configuration. There is a separate rear bumper and the windshield is tinted. There is a provision for the lighted feature. The number 1953 is molded inside the body.

1981	magnatraction lighted	☐ -4-	white/red/black
		☐ -5-	black/gold w/gold bird
		☐ -5-	black/gold w/red bird
		☐ -4-	mustard/black w/red bird
		☐ -4-	red/black w/orange bird
6200	Speed Steer	☐ -3-	white/light blue/dark blue #9
1965	magnatraction	☐ -5-	black/gold w/gold bird
1010	blazin brakes	☐ -4-	white/light blue/dark blue #2
		☐ -3-	white/light blue/black #9

Chevy Pursuit Car with Overhead Roof Lights 1979-83

The Chevy is a one piece molded body with separate front and rear chrome plated bumpers and a tinted windshield. There is a alternating flashing light mechanism mounted on the chassis to simulate a cop car in pursuit. It works very well. There were versions of the car with clear lenses and colored lights or colored lenses and clear lights. The colored light bulb variations are probably the first. There are Fire Chief and Canadian Mounted Police versions as well as the Sheriff and emergency rescue. There is a rear pin feature on the Stop Police vehicles. The pin fits in the chassis behind the rear carbon motor brush.

1979	magnatraction lighted	☐ -5-	yellow/blue #HY-71
		☐ -5-	white/blue #HY-71
1986	magnatraction lighted	☐ -4-	white/red/silver #FD-11 (Fire Chief's car)
1030	stop police lighted	☐ -1-	dark blue/white RCMP w/stickers
1050		☐ -3-	white/mustard/blue (state police)
1051		☐ -3-	white/red/orange (emergency rescue)
6290	speed steer	☐ -2-	white/red #S-3 (Sherrif's car)

Smokies Magnum Wagon 1976-77
Rapid Rescue 1976-77
Super Chief 1976-77
Pinto Thunderbolt 1976-77

The Magnum Wagon is a derivative of the Vega Van Gasser Funny car. It has an extended front and it is a molded one piece body. The rear bumper is chrome plated. There is a red tinted windshield. All cars are on a magna-steering chassis and were used in the battery operated Scre-e-echers Sets. The Rapid Rescue is a derivative of the Vega Van Gasser Funny car. It has an extended front and it is a molded one piece body. The rear bumper is chrome plated. There is a red tinted windshield. The Super Chief is a derivative of the Vega Van Gasser Funny car. It has an extended front and it is a molded one piece body. The rear bumper is chrome plated. There is a red tinted windshield. The Thunderbolt is a derivative of the Pinto Funny car. It has an extended front and it is a molded one piece body. The rear bumper is chrome plated. There is a blue tinted windshield.

5781	magna-steering	-5-	white/black #A-12
5801	magna-steering pin	-5-	white/black #A-12
5782	magna-steering	-5-	yellow/red
5802	magna-steering pin	-5-	yellow/red
5783	magna-steering	-5-	white/red with flames
5803	magna-steering pin	-5-	white/red with flames
5785	magna-steering	-4-	light blue/blue/white
5805	magna-steering pin	-4-	light blue/blue/white

Potent Pinto 1976-77
'76 Supervette 1976-77
Super 'Cuda 1976-77
Flaming 'Cuda 1976-77

The Potent Pinto is a derivative of the Pinto Funny car. It has an extended front and it is a molded one piece body. The rear bumper is chrome plated. There is a blue tinted windshield. All cars are on a magna-steering chassis and were used in the battery operated Scre-e-echers Sets. The Supervette is a derivative of the Corvette Funny car. It has an extended front and it is a molded one piece body. The blower motor, froont bumper, and driver are chrome plated. The Super 'Cuda is a derivative of the 'Cuda Funny car. It has an extended front and it is a molded one piece body. The rear bumper is chrome plated. There is a red tinted windshield. The 'Cuda is a derivative of the 'Cuda Funny car. It has an extended front and it is a molded one piece body. The rear bumper is chrome plated. There is a red tinted windshield. The flames come in different shades.

5789	magna-steering	-4-	orange/blue #22
5809	magna-steering pin	-4-	orange/blue #22
5786	magna-steering	-5-	white/red/blue #76
5806	magna-steering pin	-5-	white/red/blue #76
5790	magna-steering	-5-	orange/yellow/red #06
5810	magna-steering pin	-5-	orange/yellow/red #06
		-4-	white/blue/red Spiderman
5784	magna-steering	-5-	white/red/orange flames
5804	magna-steering pin	-5-	white/red/orange flames

Peterbilt with Trailer 1979-82

The Peterbilt is Aurora's first in the truck series. It is a one piece molded body with a separate piece rear sleeper compartment and front chrome plated grill. Provisions are made for the lighted feature. The tanks and frame are also a separate chrome plated piece as well as the (2) exhaust stacks. There are different frames and fifth wheel configurations for the auto-couple feature. The trailer can have a small pin or large pin to couple with the truck. The trailer is (2) separate pieces with opening doors on back. The Tanker is molded in two pieces.

1155	magnatraction	☐ -3-	red/mustard/yellow w/silver Shell tanker
1156	magnatraction lighted	☐ -3-	red/orange/white with silver AFX Express trailer
		☐ -3-	white/yellow/red
		☐ -3-	yellow/red/white w/Shell stickers
		☐ -2-	Crunch n Munch trailer
		☐ -2-	Chef Boy-ar-Dee trailer
1157		☐ -3-	white/blue/red with silver Aurora Racing trailer
1163		☐ -3-	white/blue/red w/trailer and race team stickers
8001		☐ -3-	yellow/red/blue RYDER

Continued on next page.

Peterbilt with Trailer 1979-82 (continued)

8003		☐ -3-	white/light blue/dark blue
6275	Speed Steer	☐ -5-	yellow/red/orange with silver AFX Express trailer
		☐ -4-	white/yellow/red w/Shell stickers
	Convoy	☐ -2-	white/light blue/dark blue w/trailer and sticker
6276		☐ -4-	white/light blue/dark blue w/Aurora Racing Trlr.
	Challenge	☐ -2-	yellow/red/orange w/trailer and sticker
6280		☐ -5-	yellow/red/orange with tanker
1175	Speed Shifter	☐ -4-	red/mustard/yellow with AFX trailer
1810		☐ -4-	red/mustard/yellow with AFX trailer

GMC Astro 95 Cab Over with trailer or tanker 1980-82

The GMC Astro is Aurora's second in the truck series. It is a one piece molded body with a separate piece front chrome plated grill. Provisions are made for the lighted feature. The tanks and frame are also a separate chrome plated piece as well as the (2) exhaust stacks. The trailer can have a small pin or large pin to couple with the truck. The trailer is (2) separate pieces with opening doors on back. The Tanker is a two piece mold.

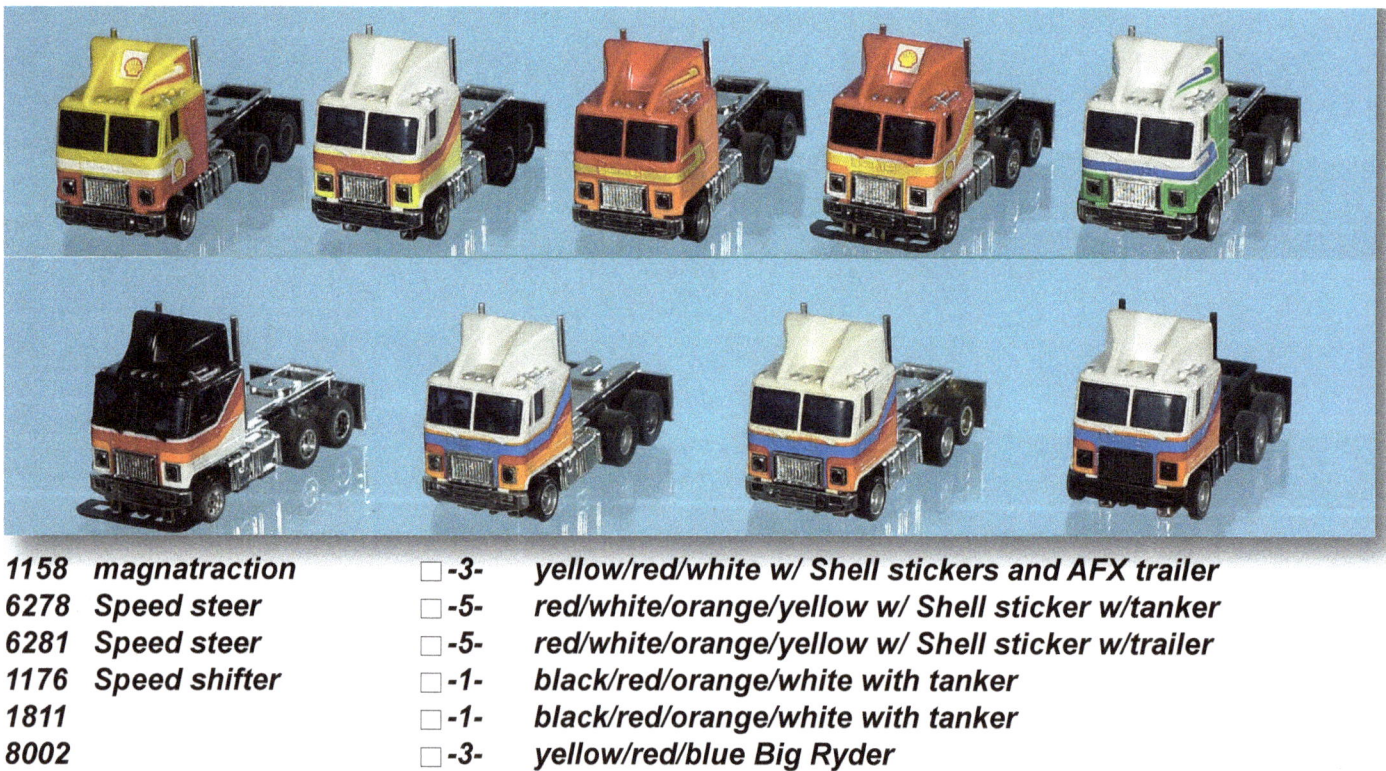

1158	magnatraction	☐ -3-	yellow/red/white w/ Shell stickers and AFX trailer
6278	Speed steer	☐ -5-	red/white/orange/yellow w/ Shell sticker w/tanker
6281	Speed steer	☐ -5-	red/white/orange/yellow w/ Shell sticker w/trailer
1176	Speed shifter	☐ -1-	black/red/orange/white with tanker
1811		☐ -1-	black/red/orange/white with tanker
8002		☐ -3-	yellow/red/blue Big Ryder
8004		☐ -4-	red/white/orange/yellow w/Shell stickers
1159		☐ -4-	white/green/blue w/silver tanker
		☐ -4-	white/green/blue w/AFX trailer
1158	magnatraction lighted	☐ -1-	black/white/red/orange w/ Shell tanker
		☐ -4-	white/blue/orange/red w/ Shell tanker
		☐ -4-	white/yellow/orange/red
		☐ -4-	red/orange/yellow

40' Ryder Auto-Couple Trailer 1982
40' Highway Auto-Couple Trailer 1982
40' Flatbed with Removable Load 1982
40' Flatbed with removable container 1982
30' Flatbed with removable container 1982
30' Flatbed with 30' Pup Trailer and (2) removable containers 1982
40' Auto-Couple Tanker 1983
Container Assortment for Big Ryder trailers 1982

These Big Ryder accessories are a match for the Ryder trucks. The trailers are two piece molded with separate doors. There is a auto-couple feature on the front wheel assembly. The low trailer is a two piece molded frame with a removable tarp covered load. The containers are removable. The pup wheel set and assembly is quite rare and very desirable today. There is also a two piece molded tanker. The auto-couple feature is attached. The containers were available as separate sale items and in a (4) pack.

8020	-3-	yellow with clear stickers
8021	-3-	silver/red
8022	-3-	red/tan load
8023	-3-	red
8024	-3-	red
8025	-1-	red with pup wheels and (2) containers
8026	-2-	chrome plated
8179	-4-	grey Seatrain
	-4-	orange OCL
	-4-	green Mitsui O.S.K. Lines
	-2-	complete Set of (4)

Examples of early AFX packaging

Assorted AFX packaging and some One Cent sale cars

AFX Big Ryder packaging and assorted carded pieces

Chapter 12
Prototypes & Promotionals

This section features the cars that Aurora was either working on and an employee had them, or they were made up as samples for the research and development team. As a collector myself, I have come across several different Aurora cars that would fit that description and several of them are photographed here for your enjoyment. There are a few cars that exist as either clear or opaque in plastic composition. As it was explained to me, these color cars were used to examine a new mold or an existing mold. They help to identify any imperfections both inside and outside. They were never supposed to be released to the public. Some have come from former employees and others have surfaced through the efforts of young dumpster divers of the '60's and 70's. Clear and opaque colored cars are shown throughout this section. Some swirl colors can be seen in different cars and these are hard to find. Usually these types of cars have virgin screw posts. It would be tough to try and collect these types of cars because some are known to be the only examples in existence. It is hard to put a rarity on them. Like all collectibles, the worth is what a willing buyer will give a willing seller.

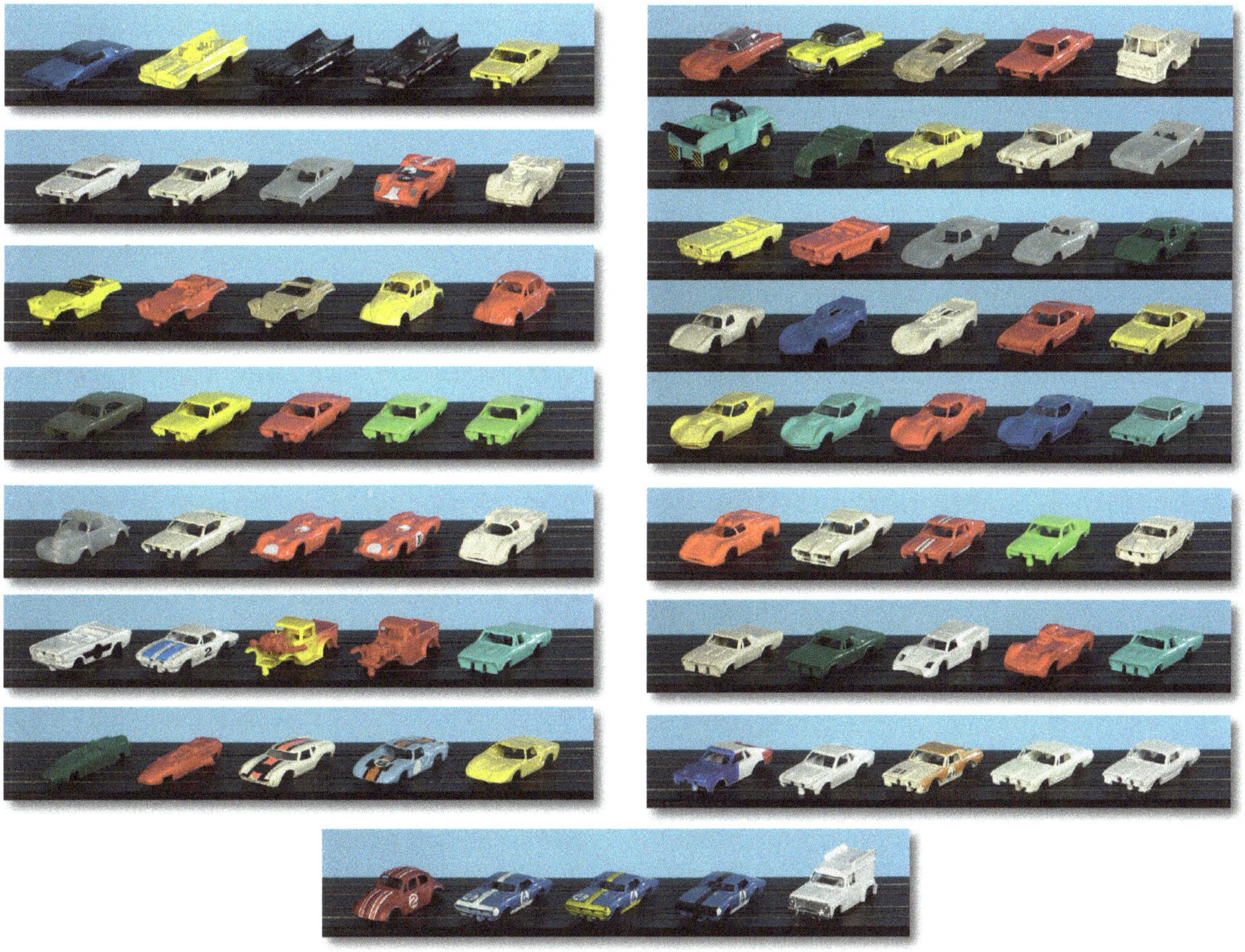

Above are shown some test shots and prototypes of what Aurora was considering before the final product hit the market.

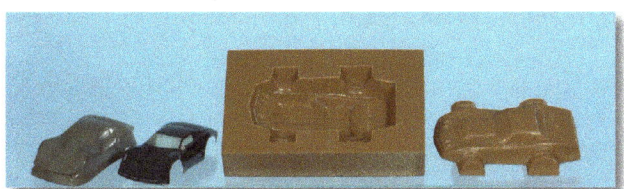

Acetate mold for a test shot body.

Banana Splits and Razzy Racer chassis.

137

Aurora Prototypes 1983

In 1983 the Aurora Products Corporation, formerly known as the Aurora Plastics Corporation, was forced to go into receivership. There are several circumstances that helped to cause the untimely demise of Aurora. These are all stories that have been substantiated to me by former employees and whether they are true or not isn't what is important here. The important matter is that the company that produced over 100 million HO slot cars since 1960, was going out of business.

In 1982 , at the Hobby Expo in Chicago, which happens a month or so before the big Toy Fair in New York, Aurora unveiled a new slot car set, Wall Climbers. A rival slot car company saw the product and proceeded to scramble to put their own version out and at the NY Toy Fair, they had a product similar to that of Aurora. A lawsuit ensued and after some time in court, Aurora lost. Not only did they loose the court case, but they lost revenues from the exclusive set they developed and they lost thousands financing the lawsuit.

Another contributing factor to Aurora's demise was the dreaded Flex track. An inventor showed them the track and they bought into it. They made a working prototype and showed it at Toy Fair. They were so confident in it's success that they put it in quite a few of their new sets for 1982. They sold thousands of pre orders and the tight tolerance molds were commissioned to be made. Several tooling problems ensued and the product was not ready to be shipped. They lost millions in sales that Christmas holiday season and banks and creditors were hounding them for money. This poor credit rating with the banks did not help them at a time when they needed a good cash flow to keep afloat. These things, among others, were the driving forces that made Aurora lock it's doors in Stamford, Connecticut and Rexdale, Canada in the spring of 1983.

In 1983 at the NY Toy Fair in February, Aurora had a tremendous presence in the HO slot car market. Their products were second to none and the '83 catalog had some of the hottest new products Aurora was planning to bring to market. Among them were the Mash Military Set and the AFX Fire Engine Play Set. No one has ever seen a MASH Military Set, but there were (6) prototype fire engines made for the play set.

When Aurora closed it's doors, the future of the company was at an end. It is with great fortune that I am able to tell you the story of what happened to a good portion of the massive inventory that Aurora had at their sales and warehousing facility in Rexdale Canada. The following is a true story, told to me by the man who lived it, Roy Manarin. Roy did what many of us, myself included, only dream about having the chance to do. He bought out the inventory of a major slot car company. Here's the story . . . .

In the winter of 1981, Roy Manarin, living in Toronto Canada, gave his son Mark an AFX slot car set for Christmas. Sometime in 1982, Roy bought a couple of G-plus cars that didn't work that good. He noticed the package said they were from Rexdale and living close to there, he went to the address. Aurora had moved to Mississauga so he got the new address and went there. There was a 100,000 square foot warehouse with a service entrance on the side. All storage and set assembly along with packaging, was done there. Aurora gave Roy (2) free AFX G-plus cars to replace his defective ones. He started to become a regular customer at the warehouse, as the prices were cheaper than at the hobby shops. By the winter of '82. Roy had spent $500.00 on cars alone, all packaged. At the time cars were $7.00 to $10.00 each at the hobby shops. He built a big layout at home for him and his son.

In the spring of 1983, Roy went back to buy more track. Aurora was having a sale. Sets were $15.00 each. All items were piled out front. He felt he could make a profit if he bought several sets and tried selling them at a local flea market. He spent $2500.00 that day, on sets, packaged cars, and loads of accessories. He rented a spot at a hobby expo in Toronto that ran for 21 days in August. He sold HO slot car merchandise and almost sold out. Roy was told that there was going to be a big auction as Aurora had gone out of business. He attended the auction. Everything in the warehouse was to be auctioned off, from office furniture to skids of HO cars. Lots were in skids measuring 4 foot by 4 foot by 4 foot high. In just loose cars there were over 30 skids. Over 100 people attended the auction.

An Aurora shipping clerk, who Roy had befriended, pointed out to him 2 other bidders who were only interested in the slot cars. Roy got together with them and decided to bid as one and split the deal if they got it. They convinced the auctioneer to combine lots and the 30 skids of cars were bid as one and no one else was prepared to buy that much stuff. They won the bidding on the HO slot car lot and here is what they left behind. A 40' trailer of Speed Steer set returns and 20 skids of cars and trucks that another bidder had won. What they bought included six 40' trailer loads. They split it evenly into two trailer loads each.

In the fall of 1983 Roy opened up a flea market booth and sold slot cars on weekends up to 1989. His son Mark, worked on Saturdays and Roy worked on Sundays. During those six years he bought out the other 2 partners inventory and sold that also. He also contacted the bidder who won the other skids of cars and trucks. He bought that stuff for 1/2 of what the guy originally paid for it.

In the summer of 1986 Roy got a call from a friend, Gino Prezio, who had a contact at Tomy, the company who bought the Aurora AFX line. They were also warehoused in Toronto. There was leftover stuff from the Aurora Products Corp. at Tomy and if he wanted it, he had 24 hours to get it out or it was being discarded. Tomy needed the floor space for a robot toy they had just introduced. Roy rented a cube van and took out 20 skids of stuff. There were 4'x4' skids of boxes marked "historical artifacts".

Aurora Prototypes 1983 (continued)

This was Aurora's archives of research and development products. Much of the things were designed and drawn at their Stamford, Connecticut office, and sent to Canada when the company folded. There were original vellum engineering drawings of all the cars and many prototypes. There were prototype cars and test shots, along with Skittles games, HO and N gauge trains, Screechers and Rail Masters Sets. In addition there were AFX sets, packaging, 1/32 track, box art separations, office paperwork, and much, much more. He spent months packaging sets and selling stuff, but the archives prototypes and vellum engineering drawings were set aside. Roy didn't realize at the time just what he had.

Roy told me that when he bought the initial auction slot cars he didn't tell his wife. She would have been upset if she had knew he spent the next 6 months of house money on slot cars (I know the feeling). He told her that the stuff was already sold. Risky, but the move paid off for him.

This preservation of the legacy of the Aurora Products Corporation of Canada, allows us to be able to document precisely, the end of Aurora. In addition, because these artifacts were saved, we were able to learn of the future direction of Aurora's AFX line and how it never was to be. The contribution that Roy Manarin has made for the hobby, will live on and on, and be retold for many years to come.

LEFT: **Hand painted trucks and cars from the 1979 catalog. Hand built prototypes and push cars.**
ABOVE: **Push cars slated for the English market.**
BELOW: **Masking process of the Porsche 934 Turbo.**
BOTTOM LEFT: **More push cars for England.**

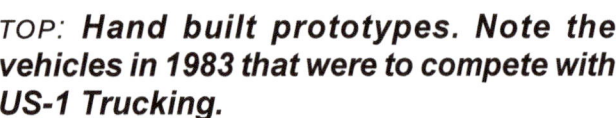

TOP: **Hand built prototypes. Note the vehicles in 1983 that were to compete with US-1 Trucking.**

TOP RIGHT: **More prototypes. Note the demolition derby cars, Bonnie and Clyde set cars (complete with bullet holes), and military pieces.**

RIGHT: **Many colors of the BMW M1 and some test shots.**

BOTTOM: **Aurora's venture into the lucrative HO train market.**

Above are shown some 2:1 patterns of some of the AFX cars with their production cars next to them. Other patterns are of cars never made.

Promotional materials.

Aurora provided dealers with the best in promotional materials throughout the years. The following are a few examples of those materials. In most cases, they were provided free of charge along with stock ordering requirements.

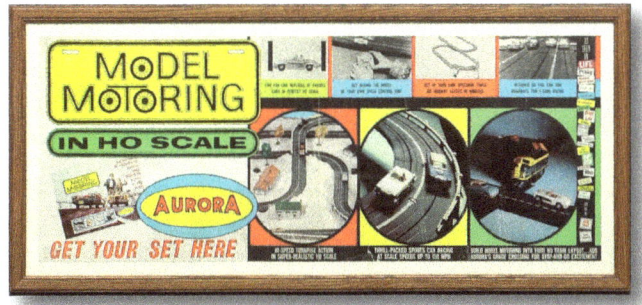 

Early '60's vibrator posters. Note the Playcraft Highways vehicles.

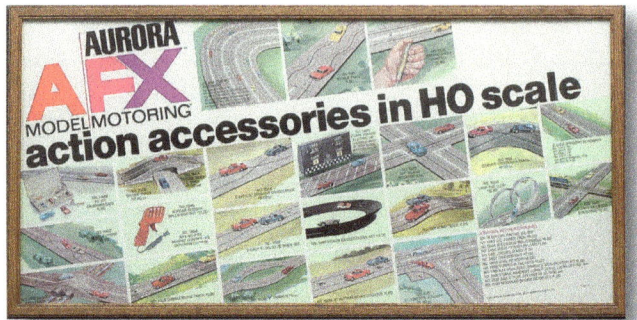

ABOVE, LEFT, AND BELOW: **Store banners and posters. The top (2) are tri-fold cardboard posters over 3 ft. long.**

BELOW: **Corn Flakes vibrator promo.**
RIGHT: **Salesman's cases for T'jets and AFX.**

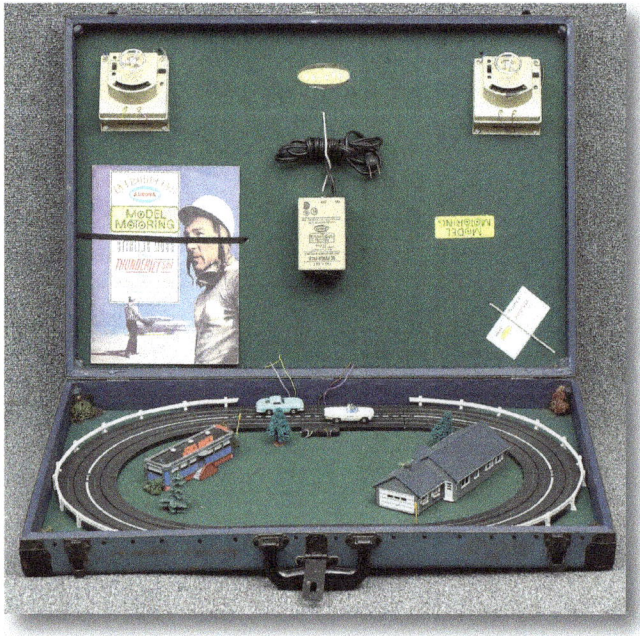

TOP: **Thunderjet display case.**
RIGHT: **AFX tee shirt promotional program.**
BOTTOM: **Several different AFX display cases.**

Chapter 13
Track & Accessories

Aurora made a whole host of track pieces and accessories to go with the Model Motoring sets. This probably accounted for the fact that Aurora was unquestionably the most popular HO manufacturer around. In 1960 their catalog was filled with track and accessories. The track was a pure copy of the Playcraft Highways (*see* Chapter 2). At first Aurora put the track mounting screw holes at the ends of the track, but after a few years they changed it to the middle. Different shades of black can be found for the track because Aurora wasted no plastic material. All the regrind of all the plastic went in a special hopper and was mixed and melted down to be used for track. Originally Aurora's track was meant for road courses so the straights had dashed lines and the curves had solid lines. In the late 60s Aurora eliminated the lines all together. The only track to be non black is the white Snowmobile and the yellow and orange Sand Van track. Both versions were introduced in special sets and the Sand Van track was sold separately. Some of the track and accessories are very desirable today due to their uniqueness or limited quantities.

Rating	#	Number	Description	Years
-5-	☐	14-19	Racing Oil	1963-76
-2-	☐	651	Trees	1960-62
-3-	☐	652	Colonial House	1960-62
-3-	☐	653	Ranch House	1960-62
-3-	☐	654	School House	1960-62
-3-	☐	655	Church	1960-62
-3-	☐	656	Railroad Station	1960-62
-2-	☐	657	Joe's Diner	1960-62
-0-	☐	658	Gas Station	1960-62
-5-	☐	1335	AFX Plus Controller	1976
-5-	☐	1342	AFX Safety Wall Pack w/terminal clip	1972-76
-5-	☐	1343	AFX Russkit Speed Control 45 ohm	1972-76
-5-	☐	1344	Speed Control Console	1970-71
-5-	☐	1345	Aurora-Russkit Speed Control 80 ohm	1970-76
-5-	☐	1346	Mark II Speed Control	969-70
-5-	☐	1347	Racing Speed Control	1964-76
-5-	☐	1348	Speed Control w/Reverse and Brake	1963-71
-5-	☐	1349	18 Volt DC-1 Power Pack	1963-64
-5-	☐	1349	20 Volt DC-2 Power Pack	1965-71
-5-	☐	1349	High Performance Power Pack	1972-73
-5-	☐	1350	Assorted Thunderjet Cars	1963-71
-5-	☐	1351	AFX DC-2 High Performance pack	1974-76
-5-	☐	1352	Rail and Post Set (light yellow)	1973
-4-	☐	1400	Speed Shifter Console	1980-82
-5-	☐	1420	Assorted Wild Ones Cars	1970
-4-	☐	1420	AFX Pit Case with Magnatraction Cars	1978-79
-2-	☐	1421	AFX Faster Drivers Kit with Case/Car	1978
-5-	☐	1422	AFX Data Race Control Center	1979-80
-5-	☐	1423	AFX Data Race Sound Tower	1979-80
-5-	☐	1430	AFX Data Race Computer Center	1979-80
-0-	☐	1434	MM Accessory Rack Assortment	1963-71
-0-	☐	1435	MM Car Display Assortment w/Display	1967-71
-5-	☐	1435	AFX High Performance speed Control	1976-77
-5-	☐	1436	AFX Aurora-Russkit 60 ohm controller	1976-82
-5-	☐	1437	AFX Aurora-Russkit 60 ohm Controller	1976-80
-5-	☐	1438	AFX Hand Controller/Speed Indicator	1978-82
-5-	☐	1439	AFX Revamatic Grandstand w/Sound	1975-77
-5-	☐	1440	Turn On Controller	1981
-5-	☐	1442	AFX Safety Wall Pak	976-82
-5-	☐	1444	AFX DC-2 High Performance Pack	1976-79
-2-	☐	1446	Pit Kit Carrying Case Mustang Cover	1969
-3-	☐	1448	H.O. Model Car Racing Book	1965-71
-4-	☐	1449	"Pit Kit" carrying case (8 cars)	1963-71
-2-			☐ red ☐ black ☐ lemon ☐ tan	
-3-	☐	1449	AFX Pit Kit carrying case (7 cars)	1972
-2-			☐ black ☐ red ☐ yellow	
-5-	☐	1450	Start / Finish Pylons	1963-71
-5-	☐	1450	AFX Start Finish Pylons	1972-73
-5-	☐	1451	Judges Stand	1963-71
-5-	☐	1451	AFX Judges Stand	1972-73
-2-	☐	1452	Grandstand	1963-71
-2-	☐	1452	AFX Grandstand	1972-73
-2-	☐	1453	Dual Pit Stop	1964-71
-2-	☐	1453	AFX Dual Pit Stop	1972-73
-5-	☐	1454	45 ohm Russkit controller w/brakes	1971-76
-5-	☐	1455	AFX Lap Timer	1974-77
-3-	☐	1456	Curved Bleachers	1964-71
-3-	☐	1456	AFX Curved Bleachers	1972-73
-5-	☐	1457	AFX Grand Stand Revamatic Sound	1974
-0-	☐	1459	AFX Concours parts kit (pit crew)	1971
-4-	☐	1460	AFX Turn On Accessory Pack	1981-82
-5-	☐	1461	AFX Hi performance parts kit	1971-76
-5-	☐	1462	Thunderjet 500 Hop Up Kit	1964-71
-5-	☐	1463	9" Radius, 2 Lane Banked Curve Adpt	1964-69
-5-	☐	1463	AFX magnatraction Hop Up Kit	1979-83
-5-	☐	1464	AFX Pit Kit carry case with high perf	1972
-3-	☐	1465	2 Lane Remote Electric Lap Counter	1964-71
-1-	☐	1466	Automatic 4-Way Traffic Light	1964-70
-5-	☐	1466	AFX Billboard Retaining Wall	1974-82
-0-	☐	1467	Electric Drag Start Track (not made)	1964
-5-	☐	1467	Monza Banked Curve Set	1969-71
-5-	☐	1468	Monza Adapters	1969-71
-5-	☐	1469	AFX Pit Kit Carrying Case	1973-83
-0-	☐	1470	Assorted Tuff Ones Cars	1970-72
-4-	☐	1470	AFX Speed Shifters Accessory Pack	1981-82
-5-	☐	1488	AFX Pit Kit Carrying Case w/High Perf	1973-76
-5-	☐	1489	AFX Race Case with Tray	1973
-0-	☐	1490	New Tuff Ones assortment	1971-72
-5-	☐	1492	AFX Race Case with Tray quickee-loc	1974-77
-5-	☐	1493	AFX Dial Lap Counter	1978-83
-2-	☐	1495	AFX Electronic Lap Counter with Timer	1978-83
-0-	☐	1497	Flamethrower assortment	1971-72
-3-	☐	1498	AFX Combo pylons and Judges stand	1974-78
-2-	☐	1499	AFX Combo stands, pitstop, bleachers	1974-78
-5-	☐	1501	9" Wiggle Track	1968-71
-3-	☐	1501w	9" Wiggle Track Ice Track, blue tint	1971
-3-	☐	1501w	9" Wiggle Track Ice Track, green tint	1971
-5-	☐	1502	9" Double Cross	1968-71
-5-	☐	1503	9" "Y" Track	1968-71
-3-	☐	1503w	9" "Y" Track Ice Track, white	1971
-5-	☐	1504	Loop The Loop track set	1966-71
-5-	☐	1505	9" Wide Track Transition	1968-69
-5-	☐	1506	9" Cobblestone Track	1965-71
-3-	☐	1506-801	9" Cobblestone Track (yellow)	1971
-3-	☐	1206-810	(same as above–carded)	1971
-5-	☐	1507	9" Automatic Starter Track	1964-69

	#	Description	Years
-5-	☐ 1508	Bridge Track	1965-71
-3-	☐ 1508w	Bridge Track Ice Track, white	1971
-5-	☐ 1509	Country Bridge and Roadway	1965-71
-1-	☐ 1509	Duo Pack Transformer Model A-1C	1961-62
-5-	☐ 1510	Motor Pack Transformer Model A-1	1960-62
-5-	☐ 1510	Culvert Bridge with Track	1966-71
-4-	☐ 1511	AC-DC Converter	1963-69
-5-	☐ 1512	9" Bump Track	1965-71
-3-	☐ 1512-802	9" Bump Track (orange)	1971
-3-	☐ 1212-802	(same as above—carded)	1971
-5-	☐ 1513	Corner Crossover Track	1965-71
-5-	☐ 1514	9" Radius Curved Roadway 1/8 Circle	1960-71
-3-	☐ 1514w	9" Radius Curved Ice Track, white	1971
-5-	☐ 1515	5" Straight Roadway	1960-71
-5-	☐ 1516	7" Straight Roadway	1960-71
-3-	☐ 1516w	7" Straight Roadway Ice Track, white	1971
-5-	☐ 1517	9" Straight Roadway	1960-71
-3-	☐ 1517-801	9" Straight Roadway (yellow)	1971
-3-	☐ 1217-801	(same as above—carded)	1971
-3-	☐ 1517w	9" Straight Roadway Ice Track, white	1971
-5-	☐ 1518	6" Radius Curved Roadway	1960-71
-3-	☐ 1518w	6" Radius Curved Ice Track, white	1971
-3-	☐ 1518o	6" Radius Curved Sand Track, yellow	1971
-5-	☐ 1519	9" Radius Curved Roadway	1960-71
-3-	☐ 1519w	9" Radius Curved Ice Track, white	1971
-3-	☐ 1519-801	9" Radius Curved Roadway (yellow)	1971
-3-	☐ 1219-801	(same as above—carded)	1971
-5-	☐ 1520	9" Terminal Straight Roadway	1960-71
-3-	☐ 1520w	9" Terminal Straight Ice Track, white	1971
-5-	☐ 1521	9" Junction Turnoff	1960-71
-3-	☐ 1522	Railroad Crossing	1961-71
-5-	☐ 1523	90 degree Intersection	1964-71
-5-	☐ 1524	9" 2 Lane Crisscross Roadway	1962-71
-3-	☐ 1525	Service Road Turnoff (pair)	1962-69
-5-	☐ 1526	Lap Counter	1964-71
-5-	☐ 1527	6" Straight track	1964-71
-4-	☐ 1528	12" Radius Crv (2) Lane (1/8 Sec.)	1964-71
-3-	☐ 1528w	12" Radius Crv (2) Lane Ice white	1971
-5-	☐ 1529	Trestle Post Ext. org, gry, butterscotch	1962-76
-5-	☐ 1530	Trestle Posts org, gry, butterscotch	1960-76
-5-	☐ 1531	Roadway Joiner and Lock Set	1960-78
-5-	☐ 1532	Rail and Rail Post Set (wht, ylw, or blk)	1960-72
-5-	☐ 1532	AFX Snap On Guard Rail (wht or ylw)	1973-82
-5-	☐ 1533	Speed Control	1960-62
-4-	☐ 1533	15" Radius Curved (2) Lane	1966-71
-3-	☐ 1533w	15" Radius Curved (2) Lane Ice white	1966-71
-1-	☐ 1534	6" Radius Curved Single Lane	1962-69
-3-	☐ 1535	5" Straight Single lane Roadway	1962-69
-3-	☐ 1536	7" Straight Single Lane Roadway	1962-69
-3-	☐ 1537	9" Straight Single Lane Roadway	1962-69
-3-	☐ 1538	9" Terminal Straight Single Lane	1962-69
-5-	☐ 1539	9" 2 Lane Squeeze Track	1964-71
-0-	☐ 1540	Assorted Model Motoring Cars	1962
-5-	☐ 1540	6" Radius Curved (1/8 Sec.) 2 Lane	1968-71
-5-	☐ 1541	9" Blow Out Track Section	1969-71
-5-	☐ 1542	15" Straight (2) Lane Roadway	1969-71
-3-	☐ 1542o	15" Straight (2) Lane sand track, org	1971
-5-	☐ 1544	AFX Speed Shifter Control (Diag Ctr)	1971-73
-5-	☐ 1544	Guard Rail (push in type)	1979
-5-	☐ 1545	Lane Stripes Red and Green	1969
-4-	☐ 1545	AFX Weight Analyzer (Diagnostic Ctr)	1971-73
-4-	☐ 1546	AFX Tire Balancer (Diagnostic Ctr)	1971-72
-4-	☐ 1547	AFX Dyno Tach (Diagnostic Ctr)	1971-73
-5-	☐ 1555	Clip On Terminal	1969-77
-3-	☐ 1555	Clip On Terminal Sand Track orange	1971
-2-	☐ 1549	AFX Diagnostic Center Assortment	1972-73
-5-	☐ 1556	Single Lane Roadway Joiner/ Lock Set	1964-70
-5-	☐ 1557	(2) Lane Lock Set (18 pcs.)	1967-71
-3-	☐ 1558	Converter Set w/ #1511, #1348, #1520	1963-69
-5-	☐ 1565	Track Elevation Supports	1976-82
-4-	☐ 1580	AFX Model Motor Handbook for 1974	1974-75
-4-	☐ 1582	AFX Model Motor Handbook Volume II	1976-77
-4-	☐ 1583	AFX Model Motor Handbook Volume III	1978-81
-5-	☐ 1587	AFX Modular bridge beam assortment	1974-78
-2-	☐	Offset bridge beams for banked turns	1970
-5-	☐ 1589	AFX Combination Tool and Circuit Test	1974-78
-5-	☐ 1590	AFX Quikee-Loc track and Car Tool	1973
-5-	☐ 1591	Modular Bridge Posts gray, orn, brsch	1967-76
-5-	☐ 1592	Modular Bridge Beams gry, orn, brsch	1966-73
-5-	☐ 1593	Daredevil Obstacle Course	1966-75
-5-	☐ 1594	Cobra Climb Spiral Roadway	1965-75
-5-	☐ 1595	AFX Modular bridge beams 3"	1974-76
-3-	☐ 1596	Vibrator Car Hop Up Kit	1962
-5-	☐ 1597	9" Speed Corners	1965-69
-5-	☐ 1598	6" Speed Corners	1965-69
-5-	☐ 1599	Modular Br Bms 6" Wide gry, orn, bsch	1967-76

"O" Gauge Track and Accessories

	#	Description	Years
-5-	☐ 1826	6" Straight Super Model Motoring Rdwy	1963-69
-5-	☐ 1827	9" Straight Super Model Motoring Rdwy	1963-69
-5-	☐ 1828	9" Terminal Straight Super M M Rdway	1963-69
-5-	☐ 1830	15" Radius Curve (1/8 cir.) Super M M	1963-69
-5-	☐ 1832	9" Squeeze Track	1964-69
-5-	☐ 1833	9" Crisscross Track	1964-69
-5-	☐ 1840	Super Model Motoring Trestle Posts	1963-69
-5-	☐ 1841	Modular Bridge Beams 4 1/2" wide	1967-69
-0-	☐ 1750	Assorted 0 Gauge Cars	1963-69

AFX Accessories

	#	Description	Years
-0-	☐ 1749	AFX car assortment	1974
-0-	☐ 1750	AFX car assortment	1971-74
-0-	☐ 1770	AFX car assortment w/ track	1972-74
-0-	☐ 1779	AFX (1973) new car assortment	1973-74
-0-	☐ 1780	AFX G-Plus car assortment	1977
-0-	☐ 1785	AFX specialty car assortment	1973-74
-0-	☐ 1790	AFX car assortment w/ track	1972-74
-0-	☐ 1795	AFX dragster assortment	1973-74
-1-	☐ 1796-500	36 car Steering Wheel Display Unit	1973-74
-0-	☐ 1960	AFX magnatraction car assortment	1977
-0-	☐ 1983	AFX magnatraction car assortment	1977
-0-	☐ 1985	AFX magnatraction car assortment	1977
-0-	☐ 1991	AFX magnatraction car assortment	1975-76
-0-	☐ 1992	AFX magnatraction car assortment	1975-76
-0-	☐ 1993	AFX magnatraction car assortment	1975-76
-0-	☐ 1994	AFX magnatraction car assortment	1975-76
-0-	☐ 1995	AFX magnatraction car assortment	1975-76
-0-	☐ 1996	AFX magnatraction car assortment	1975-76
-0-	☐ 1997	AFX magnatraction car assortment	1975-76
-0-	☐ 1998	AFX magnatraction dragster assort	1975-76
-5-	☐ 2020	AFX Start/Finish Pylon Set	1980-83
-5-	☐ 2022	AFX Judges Stand	1980-83

-2- ☐ 2023	AFX Dual Pit Stop	1980-83
-2- ☐ 2024	AFX Grandstand	1980-83
-3- ☐ 2027	AFX Bleachers	1980-83
-3- ☐ 2465	2 Lane Remote Electric Lap Counter	1972-73
-5- ☐ 2467	*Monza Banked Curve Set*	*1972-83*
-5- ☐ 2501	9" straight wiggle track	1972-83
-5- ☐ 2502	9" straight double cross track	1972-83
-5- ☐ 2503	9" "Y" Track	1972-79
-5- ☐ 2504	Loop The Loop track set	1972-82
-5- ☐ 2506	9" Cobblestone Track	1972-82
-5- ☐ 2513	Corner Crossover Track	1972-82
-5- ☐ 2514	9" Radius Curved Roadway 1/8 Circle	1972-83
-5- ☐ 2515	5" Straight Roadway	1972-79
-5- ☐ 2516	7" Straight Roadway	1972-79
-5- ☐ 2517	9" Straight Roadway	1972-83
-5- ☐ 2518	6" Radius Curved Roadway	1972-83
-5- ☐ 2519	9" Radius Curved Roadway	1972-83
-5- ☐ 2520	9" Terminal Straight Roadway	1972-73
-5- ☐ 2521	9" Junction Turnoff	1972-76
-0- ☐ 2522	Railroad Crossing (never seen)	1972-73
-5- ☐ 2523	90 degree Intersection	1972-83
-5- ☐ 2524	9" 2 Lane Crisscross Roadway	1972-82
-5- ☐ 2525	Lap Counter	1974-77
-5- ☐ 2526	9" Lap Counter	1973-82
-5- ☐ 2527	6" Straight track	1972-83
-4- ☐ 2528	12" Radius Curved (2) Lane Roadway	1972-83
-5- ☐ 2531	Shut Off Road	1979-83
-5- ☐ 2532	Flex Track	1979-83
-4- ☐ 2533	15" Radius Curve track 1/8 circle	1972-83
-5- ☐ 2534	AFX 9" Terminal Track	1976-78
-5- ☐ 2535	AFX 15" Terminal Track	1976-78
-5- ☐ 2536	AFX 9" straight Terminal Track	1979-82
-5- ☐ 2537	AFX 15" straight Terminal Track	1979-82
-5- ☐ 2538	Turn On 15" Terminal Track	1981-82
-5- ☐ 2539	9" straight squeeze tracks	1972-83
-5- ☐ 2540	6" Radius Curved (1/8 Sec.) 2 Lane	1972-83
-5- ☐ 2542	15" Straight (2) Lane Roadway	1972-83
-5- ☐ 2543	Banked "S" Curve Set	1972-78
-5- ☐ 2543	18" Flex Track	1981-83
-4- ☐ 2544	Banked Hairpin Curve	1972-74
-4- ☐ 2545	Daytona Banked Curve Set	1972-83
-5- ☐ 2546	9" Radius Curved track	1972-73
-5- ☐ 2546	15" Straight Track Pack (4 sections)	1973-76
-5- ☐ 2547	9" Curved Track Pack (4 sections)	1973-76
-5- ☐ 2550	Starter Track 15"	1974-83
-4- ☐ 2551	9" straight adapter tracks (pair)	1972-83
-4- ☐ 2552	Radar Trap w/camouflage	1981-83
-5- ☐ 2553	9" Radar Patrol w/9" straight	1982
-4- ☐ 2553	Stop Police/Blazin' Brakes Controller	1982
-5- ☐ 2555	Dragster Xmas Tree	1973-78
-5- ☐ 2556	Track and Accessory Expand-A-Set	1974-76
-5- ☐ 2557	High Speed Banked Crv Expand-A-Set	1974-76
-5- ☐ 2557	Lazer 2000 Transition Track	1983
-5- ☐ 2558	Lazer 2000 9" Straight	1983
-5- ☐ 2559	Lazer 2000 9" Radius 1/4 Curve	1983
-4- ☐ 2561	Night Car and Accy Expand-A-Set	1974-76
-5- ☐ 2562	Official Maintenance and Test Kit	1974-79
-5- ☐ 2595	Track cleaning pad	1974-77
-5- ☐ 2596	Dust Rust Must Go	1974-79
-5- ☐ 2597	X2C Oiler	1974-82
-5- ☐ 5770	Scre-e-echers Wall Pak	1976-77

-4- ☐ 7011	AFX 1982 Handbook	1982
-5- ☐ 7012	Track Cleaning Fluid	1982
-4- ☐ 7013	Fall Guy Stunt Set I	1982
-4- ☐ 7014	Fall Guy Stunt Set II	1982
-4- ☐ 7015	Fall Guy Stunt Body Set	1982
-5- ☐ 9011	Glow Guard rails	1980-82
-5- ☐ 9012	AFX Maintenance Kit	1980-81
-3- ☐ 9055	AFX Landscape scenery	1981
-5- ☐ 9057	Track Repair Clips	1980-82
-5- ☐ 9058	AFX Daredevil Hazard Jump Set	1981-83
-4- ☐ 9059	AFX Over and Under Bridge scenery	1981
-4- ☐ 9060	AFX Racing Bridge 36" (Gldn Gate Br)	1981
-5- ☐ 9061	Speed Shifter 9" Terminal Track	1981

Xlerators Accessories

-5- ☐ 2544	Hairpin Curve	1975
-5- ☐ 2712	Xlerators II wall pack	1976
-5- ☐ 2715	Xlerators II AC Transformer	1976
-5- ☐ 2716	Hairpin Curve	1976
-5- ☐ 2717	Xlerators II variable speed controller	1976
-5- ☐ 2719	9" plug in Terminal Track	1976
-5- ☐ 2720	(3) piece Banked Curve Set	1973-76
-5- ☐ 2721	15" Radius Curve "A" (pair)	1973-76
-5- ☐ 2722	15" Radius Curve "B" (pair)	1973-76
-5- ☐ 2723	6" Radius Curve (pair)	1973-76
-5- ☐ 2724	9" Straight Track	1973-76
-5- ☐ 2727	18" Straight Track (pair)	1973-76
-5- ☐ 2728	9" Terminal Track	1973-75
-5- ☐ 2729	XL AC Transformer	1973-75
-5- ☐ 2731	XL Powerpulse Control	1973-75
-5- ☐ 2732	12" Radius Curve "A" (pair)	1974-76
-5- ☐ 2733	12" Radius Curve "B" (pair)	1974-76
-5- ☐ 2734	9" Radius Curve "A" (pair)	1974-76
-5- ☐ 2735	9" Radius Curve "B" (pair)	1974-76
-5- ☐ 2736	Loop the Loop Track	1974-75
-5- ☐ 2738	Demolition Intersection	1974-76
-5- ☐ 2748	Xlerator Wall Pack	1974-75

Ultra 5 Accessories

-5- ☐ 3040	Ultra 5 car assortment	1977-78
-5- ☐ 3051	Power Pack	1977-78
-5- ☐ 3061	Steer-a-con Controller with plug	1977-78
-5- ☐ 3101	Track Elevation Support Assortment	1977-78
-5- ☐ 3102	Oil Slick Detour	1977-78
-5- ☐ 3103	Chicanes and Pylon Obstacles	1977-78
-5- ☐ 3104	LED Timing Tower with 15" Track	1978
-5- ☐ 3151	15" Straight Track	1977-78
-5- ☐ 3152	9" Radius 1/4 curve track	1977-78
-5- ☐ 3153	15" Pit area Track with 15" straight	1977
-5- ☐ 3155	Intersection with Overpass Bridge	1978
-5- ☐ 3156	Break Out Wall	1978
-5- ☐ 3157	Working Pit Stop with 15" Track	1978

Speed Steer Accessories

-5- ☐ 6051	15" Straight Track	1979-82
-5- ☐ 6052	9" Radius 1/4 curve track	1979-82
-5- ☐ 6054	15" Starter Terminal Track	1979-82
-5- ☐ 6055	Intersection with Overpass Bridge	1979-81

-5-	☐	6056	Break Out Wall	1979-81			**AFX Big Ryder Accessories**	
-5-	☐	6057	Hazard Canyon Bypass	981-82	-2-	☐ 8102	Right Hand Single Lane Turnoff	1983
-5-	☐	6058	Smokey Turn Around Ramp	1981	-2-	☐ 8103	Left Hand Single Lane Turnoff	1983
-5-	☐	6059	Breakneck Jump	1981-82	-3-	☐ 8115	Single Lane Truck Term w/Dead End	1982-83
-5-	☐	6060	Bash Bars Obstacle Set	1981-82	-3-	☐ 8116	Double Lane Truck Term w/Dead End	1982-83
-5-	☐	6150	Speed Steer wall Pack Transformer	1979-81	-5-	☐ 8117	9" Straight	1982-83
-5-	☐	6155	Speed Steer Controller with plug	1979-81	-4-	☐ 8118	Single Lane 9" Straight	1982-83
-5-	☐	6220	Thunderbird with ramp	1981	-5-	☐ 8119	9" Radius Curve	1982-83
-5-	☐	6221	Dodge Magnum with Ramp	1981	-4-	☐ 8120	Single Lane 7" straight	1982-83
-5-	☐	6231	Speed Steer car assortment	1979	-4-	☐ 8121	Single Lane 6" 1/8 Radius Curve	1982-83
-5-	☐	6277	Speed Steer Truck Assortment	1980	-4-	☐ 8124	Single Lane 5" straight	1982-83
-5-	☐	6301	Track Elevation Support Assortment	1979-81	-5-	☐ 8127	6" Straight	1982-83
-5-	☐	6302	Oil Slick Detour	1979	-5-	☐ 8138	9" Terminal Straight	1982-83
-5-	☐	6303	Chicanes and Pylon Obstacles	1979-80	-5-	☐ 8142	15" Straight	1982-83
-5-	☐	6304	Data Race Control Tower	1979-80	-4-	☐ 8175	Dispatch Center	1982
-5-	☐	6305	Data Race Sound Tower	1979-80	-4-	☐ 8176	Dispatch Extension	1982-83
-5-	☐	6306	Data Race Control Center	1979-80	-4-	☐ 8177	Container Term w overhead Gantry	1982
-5-	☐	9001	Speed Steer Car Assortment	1980	-2-	☐ 8178	Container Tractor	1982
-5-	☐	9002	Speed Steer Road blocker Assortment	1980	-2-	☐ 8190	Highway Bridge 15"	1982
					-5-	☐ 8191	Big Ryder Road Sign Set	1982
					-5-	☐ 8192	Highway Guard Rail Set	1982
					-5-	☐ 8199	Speed and Directional Hand Controller	1982

ABOVE AND RIGHT: **Vibrator and Thunderjet kits.**

Assorted vibrator and thunderjet track and accessories.

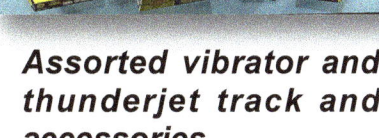

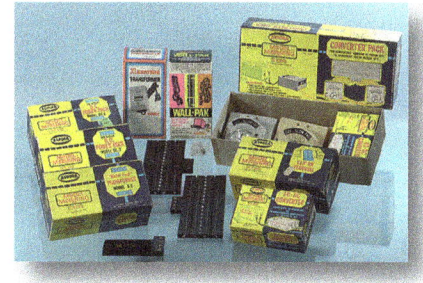

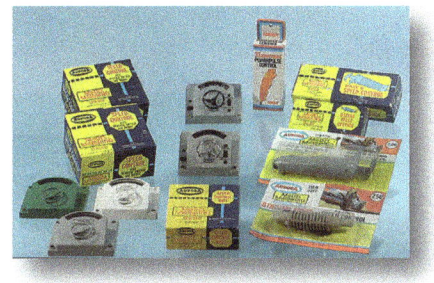

Several different AFX track and accessories.

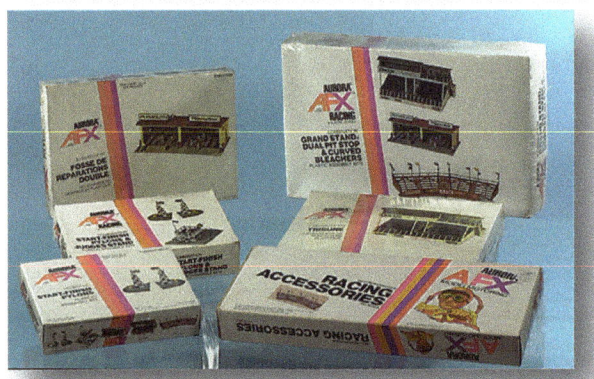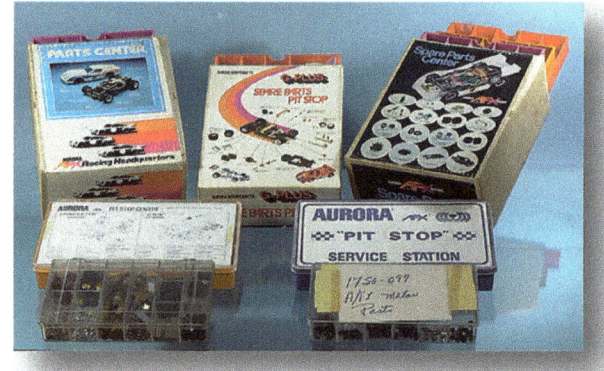

Chapter 14 Chassis

Aurora's different chassis configurations are shown here. There are also a few different variations of existing chassis. Some of those are ones with copyright dates stamped or molded into the bottom. Color variations exist and are harder to find. During the AFX years, to compete with rival slot car companies, Aurora tried several different types of slotted and slotless chassis. Today the G-Plus chassis, with slight modifications, is still being manufactured.

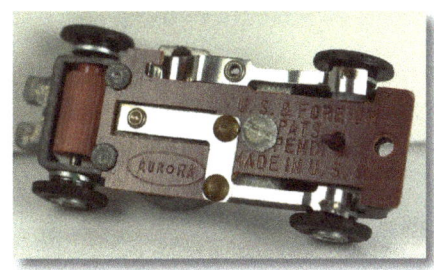

Early vibrator logo chassis. Very desirable.

ABOVE: Playcraft, vibrator, and vibrator push chassis.

RIGHT: Thunderjet, motorcycle, slimline, Wild Ones, and Tuff Ones chassis.

RIGHT: lighted tjet, O gauge, Cigarbox, and Razzy Racer chassis.

Early AFX dated chassis. Very rare.

ABOVE: **Xlerators Type 1 chassis with quadralam armatures.**

LEFT: **Xlerators Type 2 Chassis.**

RIGHT: **early AFX, magnatraction, Super II chassis.**

Specialty magnatraction chassis
(note: narrow rear tires)
rare orange chassis, prototype "dually" chassis, and non-magnatraction Specialty chassis.

Early AFX dated chassis. Very rare.

ABOVE: **Police Overheads (clear and colored lenses), MagnaSonic, and lighted magnatraction chassis.**

RIGHT: **G-Plus, G-Plus lighted, Super magnatraction, and Super G-Plus chassis.**

LEFT: **Speed Steer, Jam car, and Ultra 5 chassis.**

LEFT: **Magna steering non-pin and pin type Speed Shifter, Blazin' Brakes and Cats Eyes chassis.**

Chapter 15
Sets

Aurora featured sets in all of their catalogs and they knew it was a good way to sell add on products. They would sell exclusive sets to the large discount chains of the day like J.C. Penneys, Sears, and Montgomery Wards. These sets are called uncataloged and made up a large amount of Aurora's total sales. Some of them are very desirable today. Aurora had many famous race car drivers act as their spokesmen. Their first was Stirling Moss, who was featured on many of the Thunderjet sets. They tried to get former race car drivers because a current driver would be a detriment should an accident occur. In the 1974 AFX year, Aurora chose Peter Revson, a current driver, and he died in an untimely accident. After that, they worked with Jackie Stewart, who had recently retired.

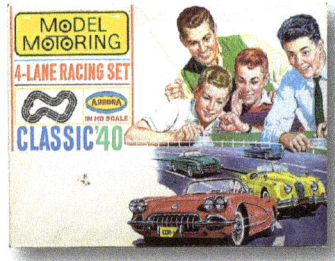

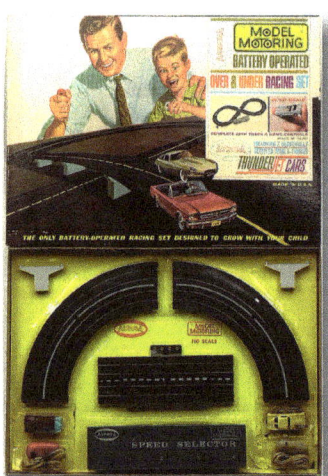
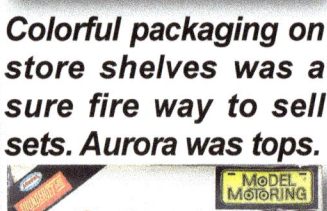

Colorful packaging on store shelves was a sure fire way to sell sets. Aurora was tops.

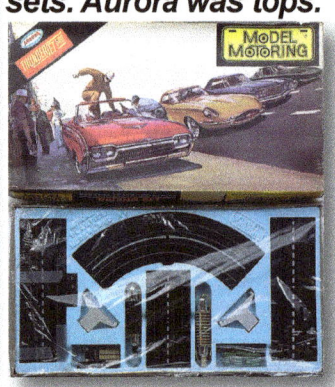

Assorted vibrator and Thunderjet sets. Check out the "Road, Race, and Rail" set and the vibrator set with the gas station and trees.

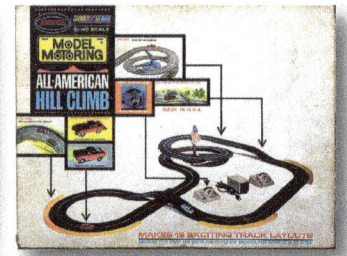

Vibrator Sets

-2- ☐ 1402	Hot Rod Drag Strip Set (has only strts)		1962
-1- ☐ 1498	4 Lane Crisscross w/Gas Sta. & trees		1962
-5- ☐ 1501	2 Lane Race Set		1960
-5- ☐ 1502	2 Lane Race Set		1960-61
-5- ☐ 1503	2 Lane Race Set		1960-62
-5- ☐ 1504	2 Lane Race Set		1960-62
-5- ☐ 1505	Classic 40 Four Lane Set		1961-62
-5- ☐ 1506	Four Lane Set		1961
-2- ☐ 1508	Scenic Special (Trees/Ranch houset)		1961
-0- ☐ 1511	Road Race Rail Set (Parkway Ind)		1961
-5- ☐ 1512	Crash Course (with intersection)		1962
-5- ☐ 1513	Classic 50 Four Lane Set		1962
-1- ☐ 1593	Aurora set marketed for HO trains		1962
-5- ☐ 1599	Crisscross Racing Set		1962

Thunderjet Sets

-5- ☐ 1300	Figure "8" Racing Set		1963
-5- ☐ 1301	Figure "8" Racing Set (no Power Pack)		1963
-5- ☐ 1301	Console 8 Race Set w/control console		1970
-5- ☐ 1302	Thunderjet Speedway Set		1963
-5- ☐ 1302	Stirling Moss Racing Set		1964-69
-5- ☐ 1303	Thunderjet Speedway Set (no Pack)		1963
-5- ☐ 1303	Console Twister Set		1970
-5- ☐ 1304	Four Lane Raceway Set		1963-66
-3- ☐ 1304	Formula 1 Whip set		1970
-5- ☐ 1305	Crisscross Racing Set		1963
-5- ☐ 1306	Championship "500" Racing Set		1963
-5- ☐ 1306	Pit Row Special Race Set		1971
-5- ☐ 1307	Figure "8" Racing Set w/steering		1964
-5- ☐ 1307	Figure "8" Racing Set w/plunger		1965-69
-5- ☐ 1308	Championship 4-Lane Set w/wheels		1964
-5- ☐ 1308	Championship 4-Lane Set w/plungers		1965-66
-5- ☐ 1308	AFX Rally 500 Race Set		1972
-5- ☐ 1310	Double 8 Racing Layout		1965-69
-2- ☐ 1311	Battery Operated Oval Racing Set		1965-69
-2- ☐ 1312	Battery Operated Over and Under		1965-69
-5- ☐ 1313	Tabletop Racing Set		1965
-5- ☐ 1314	Custom Racing Set		1967-69
-5- ☐ 1315	Continental Racing Set		1967-69
-5- ☐ 1316	International Racing Set		1967-69
-5- ☐ 1317	Championship 500 4 Lane Racing Set		1967-69
-5- ☐ 1318	Super Looper 2 Lane Racing Set		1967-69
-0- ☐ 1319	Thunderbike Racing Set (never made)		1967
-5- ☐ 1320	Wide Track 2 Lane Racing Set		1967-69
-3- ☐ 1321	Formula 1 Racing Set		1969
-5- ☐ 1322	High Banked Racing Set		1969
-5- ☐ 1323	24 Hours of Le Mans Set		1970
-5- ☐ 1324	Championship 500 (4) Lane Race Set		1970
-1- ☐ 1325	Championship High Sierra Styrofoam		1970
-4- ☐ 1326	Sand Van Set		1971
-5- ☐ 1330	24 Hours Of LeMans Race Set		1971
-5- ☐ 1333	Flamethrower Red Dunes Race Set		1971
-2- ☐ 1334	Bushwacker Snowmobile Race Set		1971-72
-5- ☐ 1422			1962
-5- ☐ 1603	Loop the Loop Set		1967
-5- ☐ 1605			1966
-5- ☐ 1608	Tabletop Racing Set 2 Lane		1967
-3- ☐ 1620	Super Skyway Race Set	Wards	1967
-5- ☐ 1623	Three Level Racing Set		1966
-5- ☐ 1629	Rally 300 Race Set		1971
-5- ☐ 1634			1966
-5- ☐ 1657		Sears	1966
-5- ☐ 1659			1966
-5- ☐ 1665	2 Lane Set		1965
-5- ☐ 1674	Over and Under Racing Set		1965
-5- ☐ 1676			1966
-5- ☐ 1677	Wide Track Special Race Set		1967
-5- ☐ 1689	4 Lane Raceway	Sears	1967
-5- ☐ 1690	Golden Gate Bridge Set	Wards	1966
-5- ☐ 1691	Golden Gate Bridge Set	Wards	1966
-5- ☐ 1694			1967
-2- ☐ 1696	Computrac Set	Sears	1966
-2- ☐ 1697	Computrac Set		1966
-5- ☐ 1776	All American Hill Climb w/flag		1965
-5- ☐ 1909	4 Lane Speedway		1968
-5- ☐ 1943	Formula I Racing Set		1969
-5- ☐ 1950	Tabletop Racing Set	Sears	1969
-5- ☐ 1972	High Bank Racing Set		1969
-5- ☐ 1978	Real Racing Featuring the Wild Ones		1970
-5- ☐ 1983	Real Racing w/ Mach I	Penneys	1970
-3- ☐	Flying Turns Set	Wards	1970

"O" Gauge Sets

-3- ☐ 1701	Super Model Motoring Oval		1963-66
-3- ☐ 1704	Super Model Motoring Figure 8		1963-66
-3- ☐ 1705	2 In 1 Racing Set		1965

AFX Sets

-5- ☐ 1327	California Oval Race Set (tjet track)		1971
-5- ☐ 1327	California Oval Race Set		1972
-5- ☐ 1328	Pit Row Special Race Se t(tjet track)		1971
-5- ☐ 1328	Pit Row Special Race Set		1972
-5- ☐ 1329	Monza Twin Race Set (tjet track)		1971
-5- ☐ 1330	24 Hours of LeMans Race Set		1972
-5- ☐ 1331	Rally Whip Race Set (tjet track)		1971
-5- ☐ 1332	Monster Four Lane Race Set(tjet track)		1971
-5- ☐ 1338	Daytona "S" Race Set		1972
-5- ☐ 1339	Road Americana Race Set		1972
-5- ☐ 1340	Monza Spider Race Set		1972
-5- ☐ 1341	Firecracker Four Race Set		1972
-4- ☐ 2001	Road Burners Super Sprint (Battery)		1977-78
-4- ☐ 2002	Road Burners Rally 2000 (Battery)		1977-78
-5- ☐ 2071	Jackie Stewart Oval 8 Race Set		1976
-5- ☐ 2072	Jackie Stewart Day and Night Enduro		1976
-5- ☐ 2073	Jackie Stewart Dual Oval Speedway		1976
-5- ☐ 2074	Jackie Stewart Pitstop Challenget		1976
-5- ☐ 2075	Jackie Stewart High Banked Set		1976
-5- ☐ 2076	Jackie Stewart Revamatic Sound Set		1976
-5- ☐ 2077	Jackie Stewart Firecracker Four Car		1976
-5- ☐ 2078	Jackie Stewart Grand Prix Royale Set		1976
-5- ☐ 2084	Jackie Stewart Natl Spdsters RAT '55		1976
-5- ☐ 2101	Daytona 500		1977
-5- ☐ 2102	12 Hrs. Of Sebring		1977
-5- ☐ 2103	Darlington 500		1977
-5- ☐ 2104	Pocono Can-Am		1977
-5- ☐ 2105	Riverside 400		1977
-5- ☐ 2106	Watkins Glen Grand Prix		1977

-5-	☐	2107	Firecracker 400	1977	-5-	☐	2612	The Demolition 8 Racing Set(2 car set)	1974
-5-	☐	2108	Monaco Grand Prix	1977	-5-	☐	2613	Big Loop Racing Set(2 car set)	1974
-5-	☐	2120	Championship Day Night Raceway	1977	-5-	☐	2614	Sideswipers IV Team Racing Set(4 car set)	1974
-1-	☐	XXXX	Japanese Tomy Race Set	1977	-5-	☐	1662	Custom High Speed Int'l IV Set (4 car) Wards	1975
-5-	☐	2162	Jackie Stewart Meadowbrook Race	1976	-5-	☐	2671	Super 8 Race Set(2 car set)	1976
-5-	☐	2163		1976	-5-	☐	2672	High Speed Demolition Set(2 car set)	1976
-5-	☐	2167		1976	-5-	☐	2673	Big Loop Demolition Speedway(2 car set)	1976
-5-	☐	2201	Riverside 500 Race Set	1972-73	-5-	☐	2674	High banked Daredevil Raceway(2 car set)	1976
-5-	☐	2202	Monte Carlo Race Set	1973					
-5-	☐	2203	Pit Row Special II Race Set	1973				***Ultra 5 Sets***	
-5-	☐	2204	Daytona 880 Race Set	1973	-5-	☐	2901	Grand Challenge Race Set	1977
-5-	☐	2205	National Speedsters Race Set	1973	-5-	☐	2902	Pro Am Classic Race Set	1977
-5-	☐	2206	Monza Marathon Race Set	1973	-5-	☐	2903	Futura 500 Race Set	1977
-5-	☐	2207	Firecracker 4+4 Race Set	1973	-5-	☐	2911	Can Am Classic Race Set	1978
-4-	☐	2211	Peter Revson Phoenix 500 Race Set	1974	-5-	☐	2913	Super Cyclone 500 Race Set	1978
-4-	☐	2212	Peter Revson Pit Row Speedway	1974	-5-	☐	2914	Championship Royale Race Set	1978
-4-	☐	2213	Peter Revson Racemaster Challenger	1974					
-4-	☐	2214	Peter Revson Revamatic 500 Race Set	1974				***Speed Steer Slotless Racing Sets***	
-4-	☐	2215	Peter Revson California National Race	1974	-5-	☐	5821	Speed Steer Enduro Race Set	1979
-4-	☐	2216	Peter Revson Rallye 4+4 Race Set	1974	-5-	☐	5822	Speed Steer Convoy Challenge Race Set	1979
-4-	☐	2217	Peter Revson Grand Royale Race Set	1974	-5-	☐	5823	Speed Steer Road Blocker Race Set	1979
-5-	☐	2230	Jackie Stewart Oval 8 Race Set	1975	-5-	☐	5821	Speed Steer Data Race I Race Set	1979
-5-	☐	2231	Jackie Stewart Night Lights Race Set	1975	-5-	☐	5822	Speed Steer Data Race II Race Set	1979
-5-	☐	2232	Jackie Stewart High Bank Challenge	1975					
-5-	☐	2233	Jackie Stewart Revamatic Competition	1975				***Scre-e-echers Sets*** (all injection molded ready to race)	
-5-	☐	2234	Jackie Stewart Universal High Speed	1975	-3-	☐	5751	Thrill Show (single track)	1976
-5-	☐	2235	Jackie Stewart Championship Four Set	1975	-3-	☐	5752	Interstate chase set	1976
-5-	☐	2236	Jackie Stewart Grand Royale Set	1975	-3-	☐	5753	Drag City Race Set	1976
-5-	☐	2239		1974	-3-	☐	5755	Fireman's Thrill Show	1977
-5-	☐	2304		1979	-3-	☐	5756	Interstate Chase Set	1977
-1-	☐	2306	Monza Sprint Sears Super Traction	1974	-3-	☐	5757	Spiderman Meets the Fly Race Set	1977
-5-	☐	2309		1973	-3-	☐	5758	Drag City Race Set	1977
-5-	☐	2311	Blazer 500 Race Set	1979					
-5-	☐	2441	Road Atlanta Race Set	1978				***Canadian AFX Sets***	

Aurora Canada was the headquarters for the product line from 1979 to the end in 1983 when they went out of business and were bought by Tomy Toys.

-5-	☐	2442	Daytona Racing Set	1978					
-5-	☐	2443	Sebring Race Set	1978	-5-	☐	10023	Daredevil Hazard Race Set (Rebel Charger)	1981
-5-	☐	2444	Darlington Race Set	1978	-5-	☐	10041	Corvette Challenge Race Set	1981
-5-	☐	2445	Pocono Race Set	1978	-5-	☐	10042	Firebird Fever ace Set	1981
-5-	☐	2446	Riverside Race Set	1978	-5-	☐	10043	Cats Eyes Day and Night Marathon Road Set	1981
-5-	☐	2447	Road America Race Set	1978	-5-	☐	10044	Cross Country Rallye Race Set	1981
-5-	☐	2448	Watkins Glen Race Set	1978	-5-	☐	10045	Blazin' Brakes Collision Challenge Race Set	1981
-5-	☐	2449	Firecracker 400 Race Set	1978	-5-	☐	10046	Highway Pursuit Road Set	1981
-5-	☐	2450	Monaco Race Set	1978	-5-	☐	10047	Speed Shifter Super Turbo Challenge Race Set	1981
-5-	☐	2457	Silver Anniversary Corvette Set	1978	-5-	☐	10048	Stop Police Radar Chase Road Set	1981
-5-	☐	2466		1978	-5-	☐	10049	Grand Prix International Race Set	1981
-5-	☐	2701	Daytona 500 Race Set	1979	-5-	☐	10051	Data Race Computerized Race Set	1981
-5-	☐	2702	Riverside Race Set	1979	-5-	☐	10052	Speed Shifter Turbo Rig Challenge Race Set	1981
-5-	☐	2703	Mario Andretti Grand Prix Int Challenge	1979	-5-	☐	10090	Speed Steer Thrill Show	1981
-5-	☐	2704	Smokey and The AFX Express Set	1979	-5-	☐	10091	Speed Steer Maniac Madness Road Set	1981
-5-	☐	2705	Mario Andretti Grand Prix Int'l Champ	1979	-5-	☐	10092	Speed Steer Boomerang Police Chase Road Set	1981
-5-	☐	2706	Firecracker 400 Race Set	1979	-5-	☐	20001	Custom 8 Race Set	1983
-5-	☐	2707	Data Race Challenge Race set	1979	-5-	☐	20006	Corvette Challenge Race Set	1982
-5-	☐	2708	Data Race Championship Race Set	1979	-5-	☐	20009	Nite Chase America	1982
-5-	☐	6304	Data Race I Set	1979	-5-	☐	20015	King Of The Road Race Set	1982

Xlerators Sets

-5-	☐	2601	Sideswipers Set(2 car set)	1973
-5-	☐	2602	Speedblazers Set(2 car set)	1973
-5-	☐	2603	Team Racing Set(4 car set)	1973
-5-	☐	2611	Figure 8 Racing Set(2 car set)	1974

-3- ☐ 20018	Super G-Plus G.P. 1200 Race Set	1982-83
-3- ☐ 20021	Fall Guy Bounty Hunter Race Set	1983
-5- ☐ 20024	Lazer 2000 Wall Climber Race Set	1982
-5- ☐ 20027	Stop Police Radar Chase	1982
-5- ☐ 20030	Super G-Plus G.P. 1600 Race Set	1982
-3- ☐ 20033	Fall Guy Hollywood Stunt Set	1982
-5- ☐ 20039	Lazer 2000 Wall Climber II	1982
-5- ☐ 20042	Speed Shifter Super Turbo Challenge	1982
-5- ☐ 20048	Four Lane Racing Daytona	1982-83
-3- ☐ 20054	Big Ryder Intercity Hauler	1982
-3- ☐ 20057	Big Ryder Container Trucking	1982
-1- ☐ 20060	Big Ryder Interstate Express Delivery	1982
-1- ☐ 20063	Big Ryder Cross Country Dispatch	1982-83
-5- ☐ 20069	Speed Steer Thrill Show	1982
-5- ☐ 20072	Speed Steer Maniac Madness Set	1982
-5- ☐ 21002	Roarin' Rolls Royce Set	1982
-0- ☐ 30006	M*A*S*H* Military Set *(not made)*	1983
-5- ☐ 30025	Lazer 2000 Wall Climber Double Loop	1983
-0- ☐ 30066	AFX Fire Engine Play Set *(not made)*	1983
-5- ☐ 80002	Firebird Fever Race Set	1980
-5- ☐ 80003	Nite Chase Road Set	1980
-5- ☐ 80006	4X4 Lighted Blazer Rally Road Set	1980
-5- ☐ 80007	Highway Pursuit Bridge Set	1980
-5- ☐ 80008	Grand Prix International Race Set	1980
-5- ☐ 80010	Data Race Computerized Race Set	1980
-5- ☐ 80040	Speed Shifter Turbo Powered Set	1980
-5- ☐ 80041	Speed Shifter Truckers Challenge Set	1980
-5- ☐ 80080	Speed Steer Truck Road-eo Race Set	1980
-5- ☐ 80081	Speed Steer 3 car Grand Challenge	1980
-5- ☐ 80082	Speed Steer 3 Car Champion Royale	1980
-5- ☐ 90001	Figure 8 Custom Van Race Set	1979
-5- ☐ 90002	Daytona 500 Race Set	1979
-5- ☐ 90003	Rallye Race Set	1979
-5- ☐ 90004	Police Pursuit Race Set	1979
-5- ☐ 90005	Indy Special Race Set	1979
-5- ☐ 90006	AFX Overnite Express Race Set	1979
-5- ☐ 90007	High Banked Raceway	1979
-5- ☐ 90008	Golden Gate Bridge Race Set	1979
-5- ☐ 90009	Mario Andretti Grand Prix International	1979
-5- ☐ 90010	Firecracker 400 Race Set	1979
-5- ☐ 90011	AFX DataRace Set	1979
-5- ☐ 90012	Monaco Grand Prix Race Set	1979
-5- ☐ 90013	AFX Custom Van Race Set	1980
-5- ☐ 90018	AFX Firecracker 400 Race Set	1980
-5- ☐ 90026	AFX Lited Rig Police Chase Road Set	1980
-5- ☐ 90027	AFX Spiral Challenge Race Set	1980
-5- ☐ 90028	AFX Lited Oval Sprint Set	1980

Spanish AFX sets

-3- ☐ GX1100	Super 8 Set	1981-82
-3- ☐ GX1300	Flex track Figure 8 Set	1981-82
-3- ☐ GX1750	24 Hours Super Flamethrowers Set	1981-82
-3- ☐ GX2850	Stop Police Set	1981-82
-3- ☐ GX3500	Formula 1 G+Plus Set	1981-82
-3- ☐ GP4030	Grand Prix Set	1981-82
-3- ☐ GX7500	Four Lane G+Plus Set	1981-82
-3- ☐ GX8500	World Championship Set	1981-82
-3- ☐ GS500	Speed Steer Turbo Challenge Set	1981-82
-3- ☐ GS1000	Speed Steer Convoy Challenge Set	1981-82

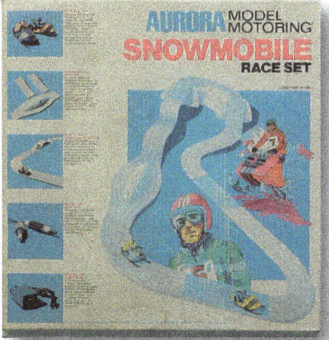

All kinds of specialty sets and gimmicks kept Aurora in the lead among HO slot car manufacturers.

AFX sets both cataloged and uncataloged.

 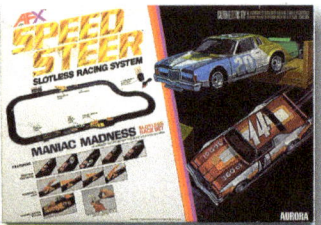  

AFX specialty sets for Speed Steer and Magna Steering.

 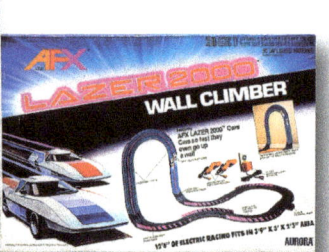 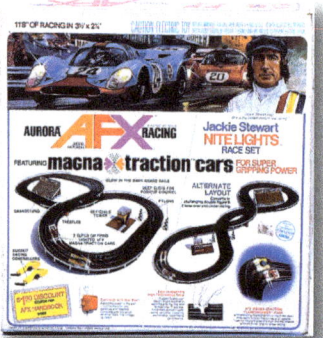 

Xlerators set along with some assorted AFX sets.

 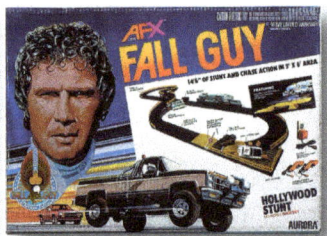 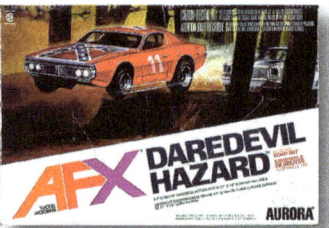 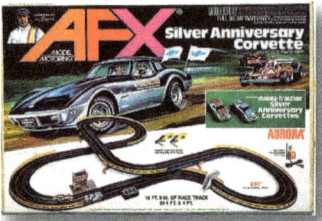

Aurora licensing of "The Fall Guy" and not licensed "Dukes" set.

Japanese Tomy set from 1977, Chef Boy R Dee set, and Big Ryder trucking.

Aurora through the years was very good at documenting their products. They did this with color and black and white catalogs and flyers. There were hundreds available for the 24 year HO slot car history of the company. We will show some of the more notable ones in this chapter. Collecting this paperwork has increased in popularity over the past few years and where some of the actual cars are prohibitive in cost, the catalogs showing them can be had fairly reasonably. The rarity of the catalogs and paperwork is rated at (-5-) for instruction sheets and most black and white flyers to (-1-) for color catalogs and most other color items.

 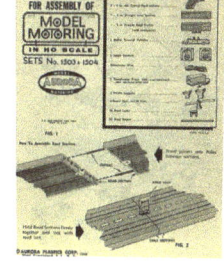 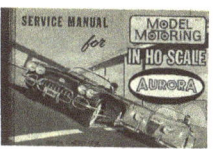  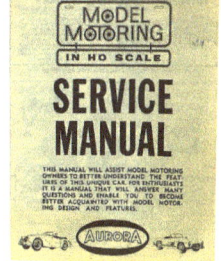

1960

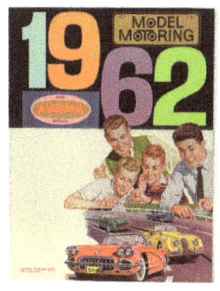    

1961

    (price list 1962)

1962

 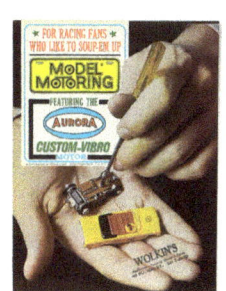  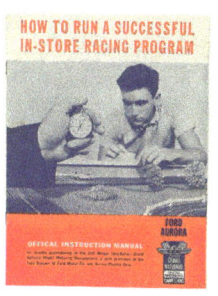 (1963 row)

1963 above, 1964 below

157

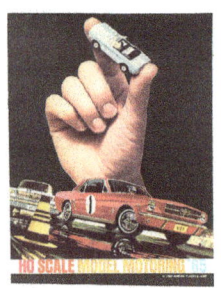  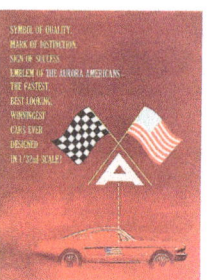  

1965

 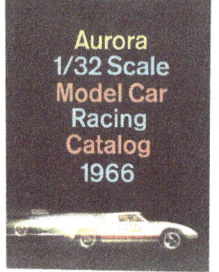  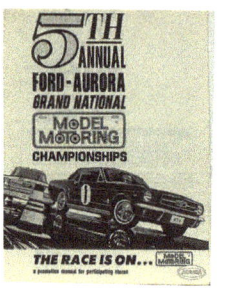 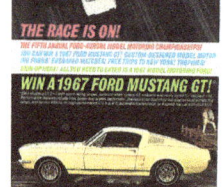

1966

    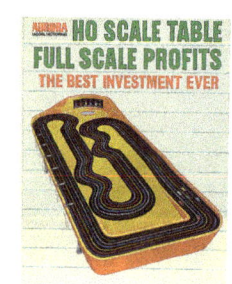

1967

1968

   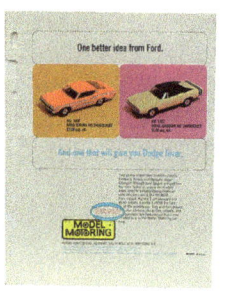 

1969

  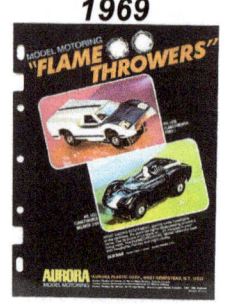  

1970

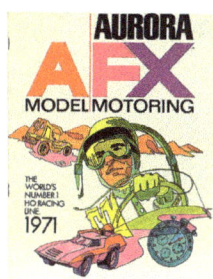  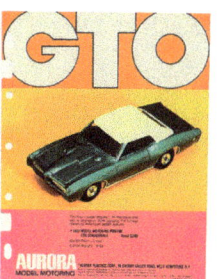 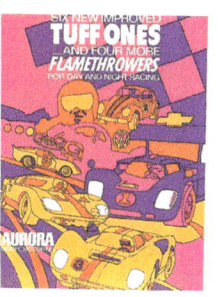 

1971

    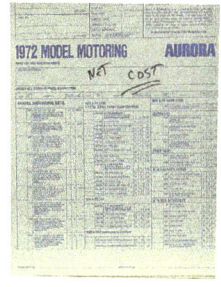

1972

 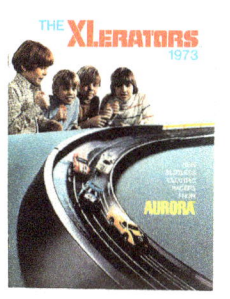   

1973

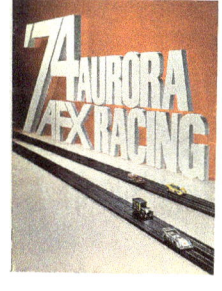 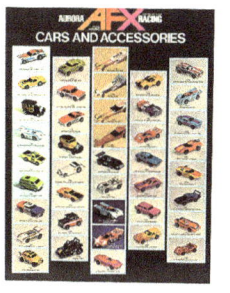   

1974

1975

    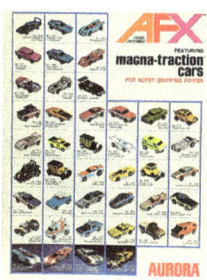

1976

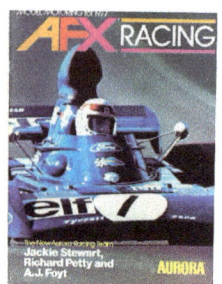  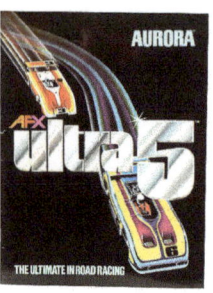  

1977

    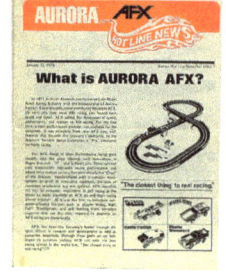

1978

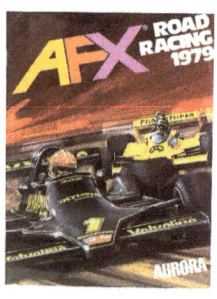    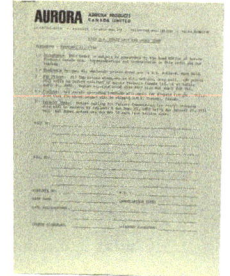

1979

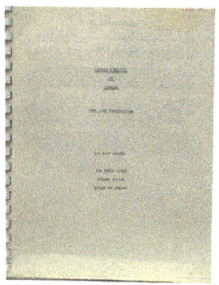  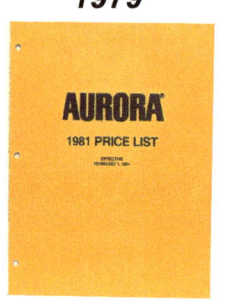 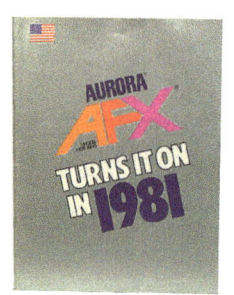 

1980 through 1982

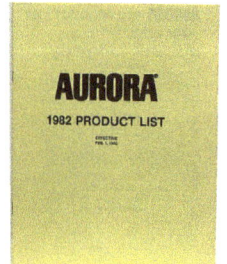 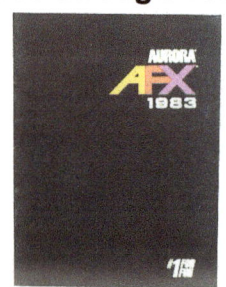 

1983

The infamous year that was to become the beginning of the end for Aurora. Their history lives on with the many products and literature that they produced.

Aurora's demise in 1983.

Here's a glimpse of what would have been manufactured...As it was on the drawing board! Notice the pieces that made it into another slot car company's product line.

See Chapter 12 for the complete story...

Aurora's Engineering Team
designed the best H.O. slot cars in the world...

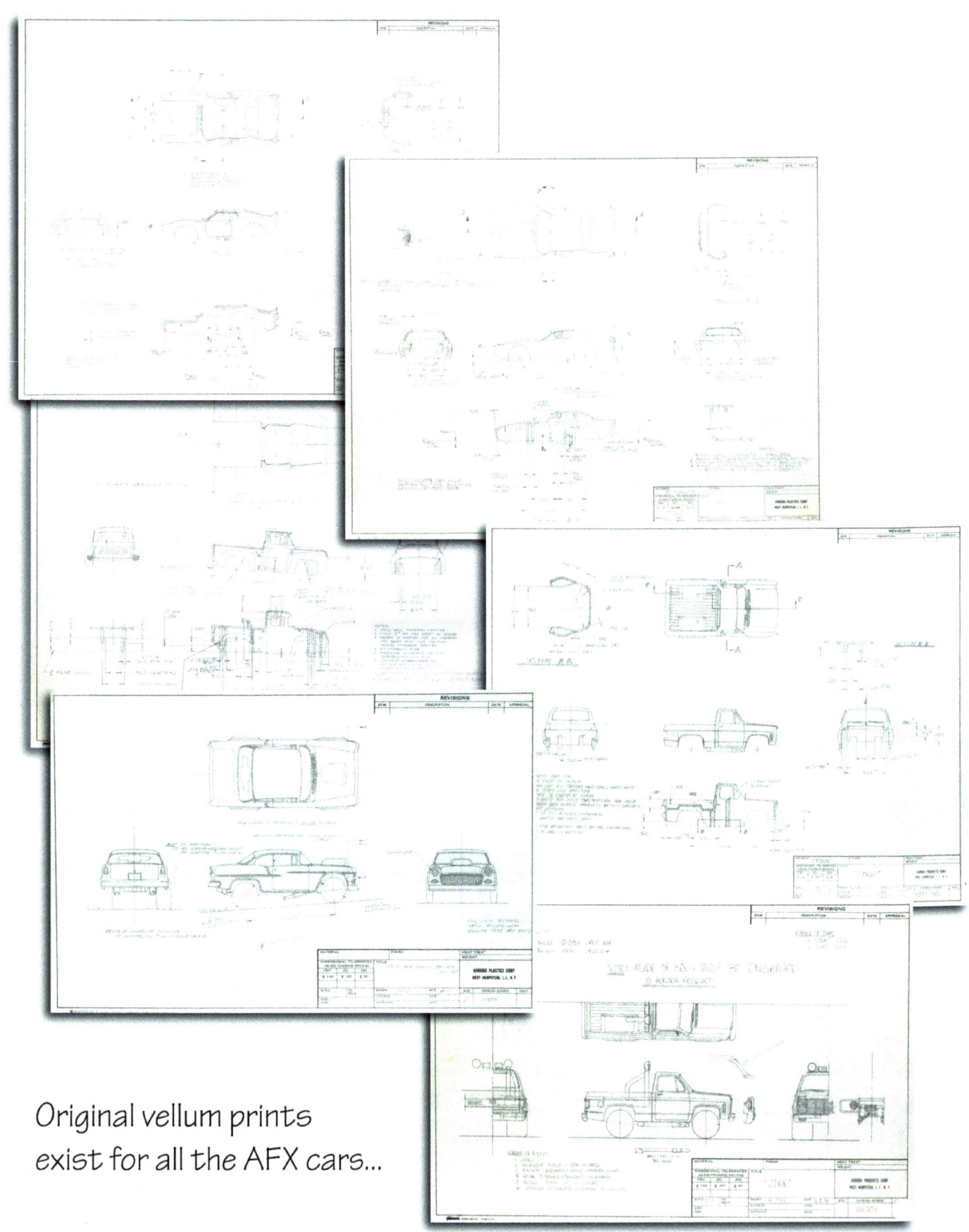

Original vellum prints
exist for all the AFX cars...

www.ingramcontent.com/pod-product-compliance
Lightning Source LLC
Chambersburg PA
CBHW061212230426
43665CB00032B/2986